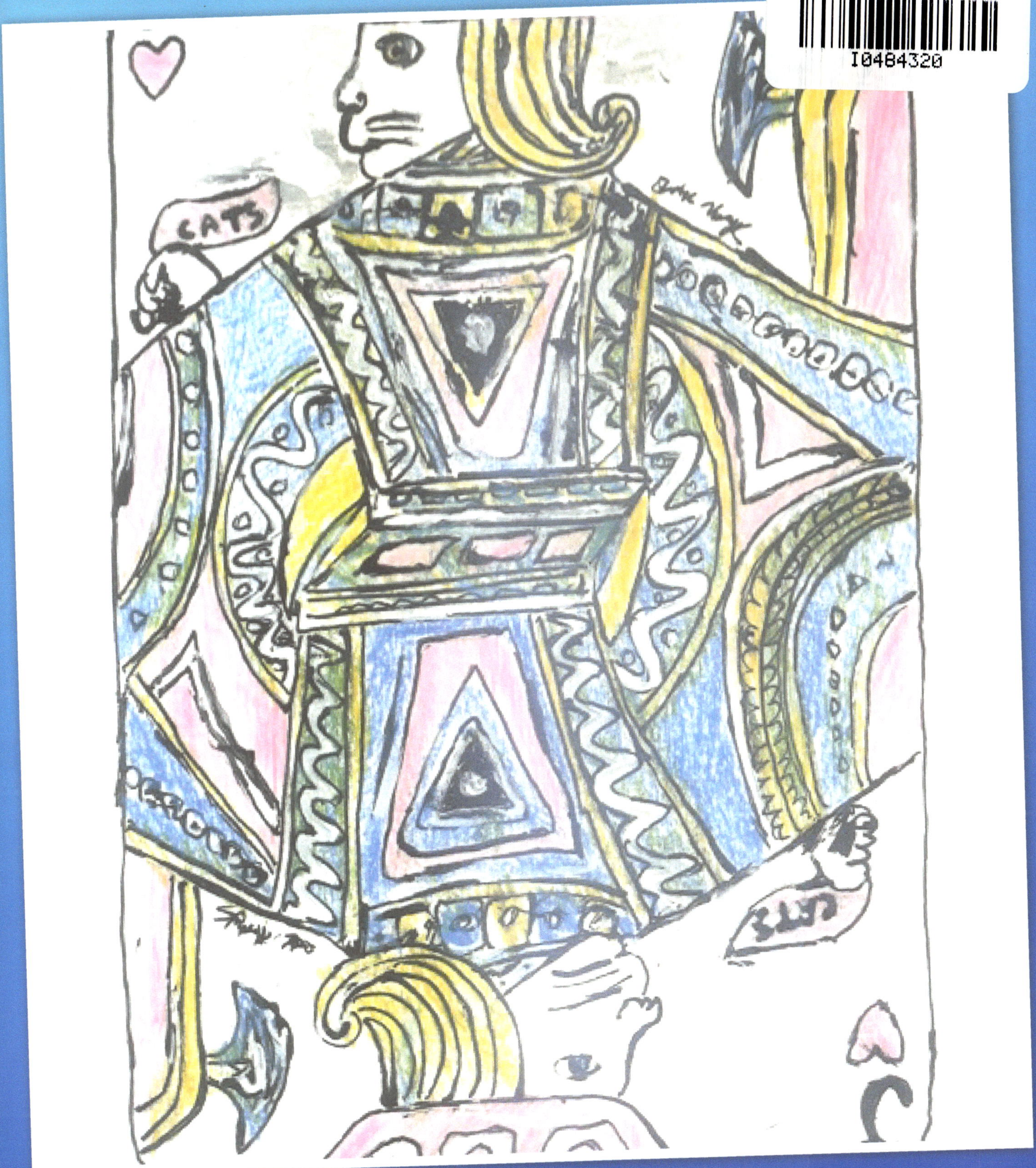

PATCATART

playing cards

PATCATART
PLAYING CARDS

IMAGES OF CAT PLAYING CARDS

ORIGINAL PAINTINGS BY
PATRICK B. HUMPHREYS

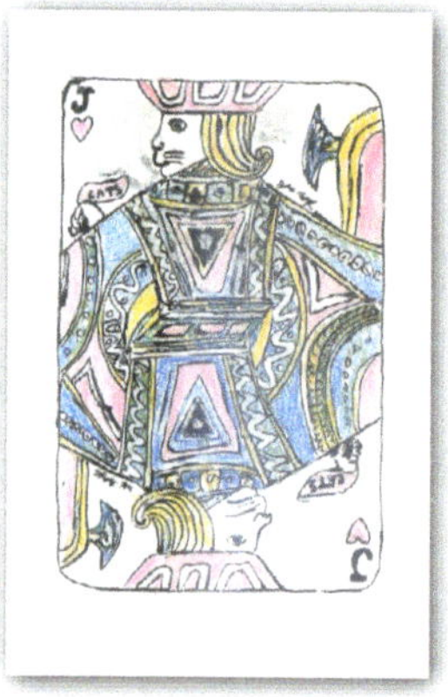

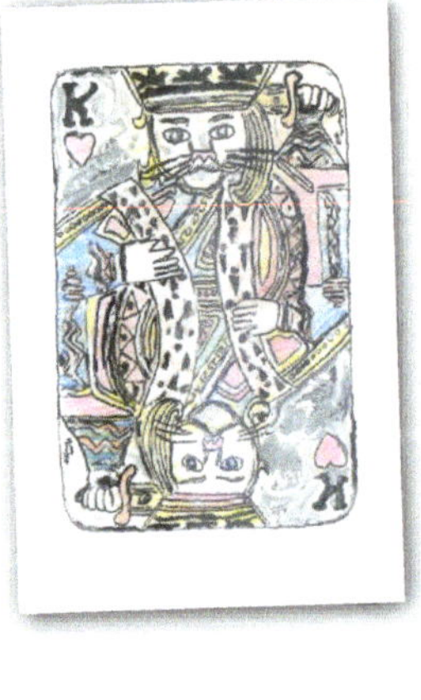

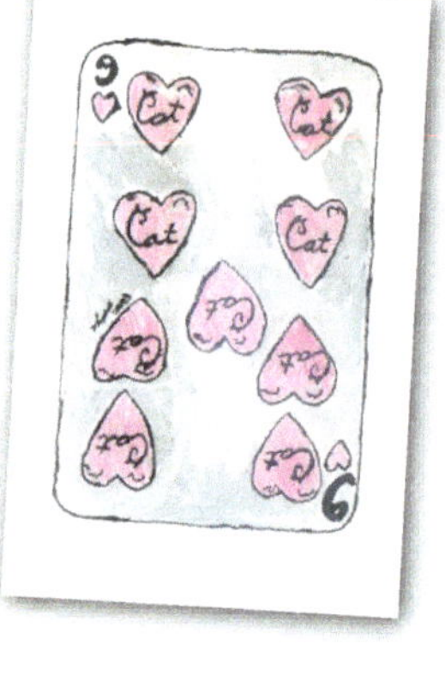

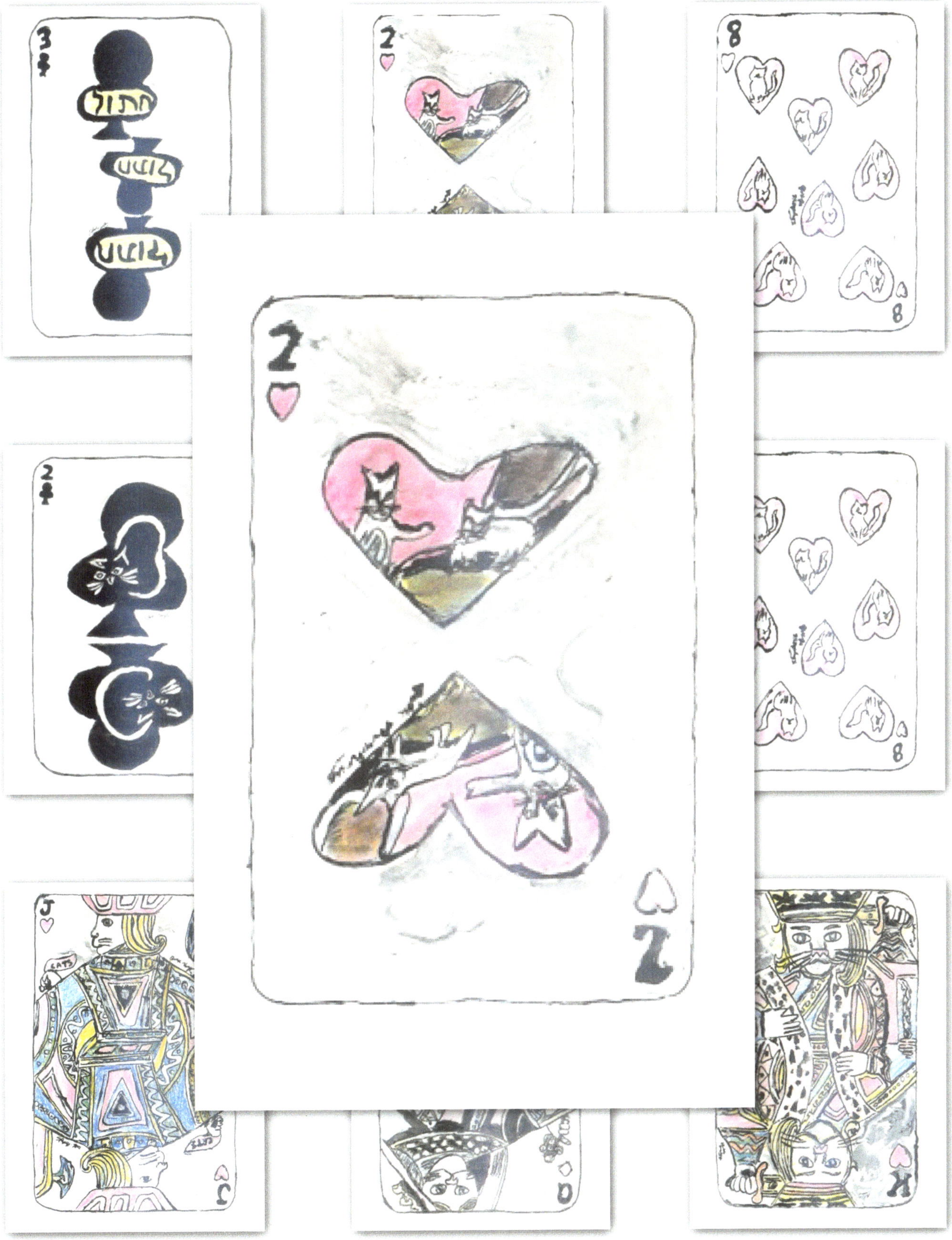

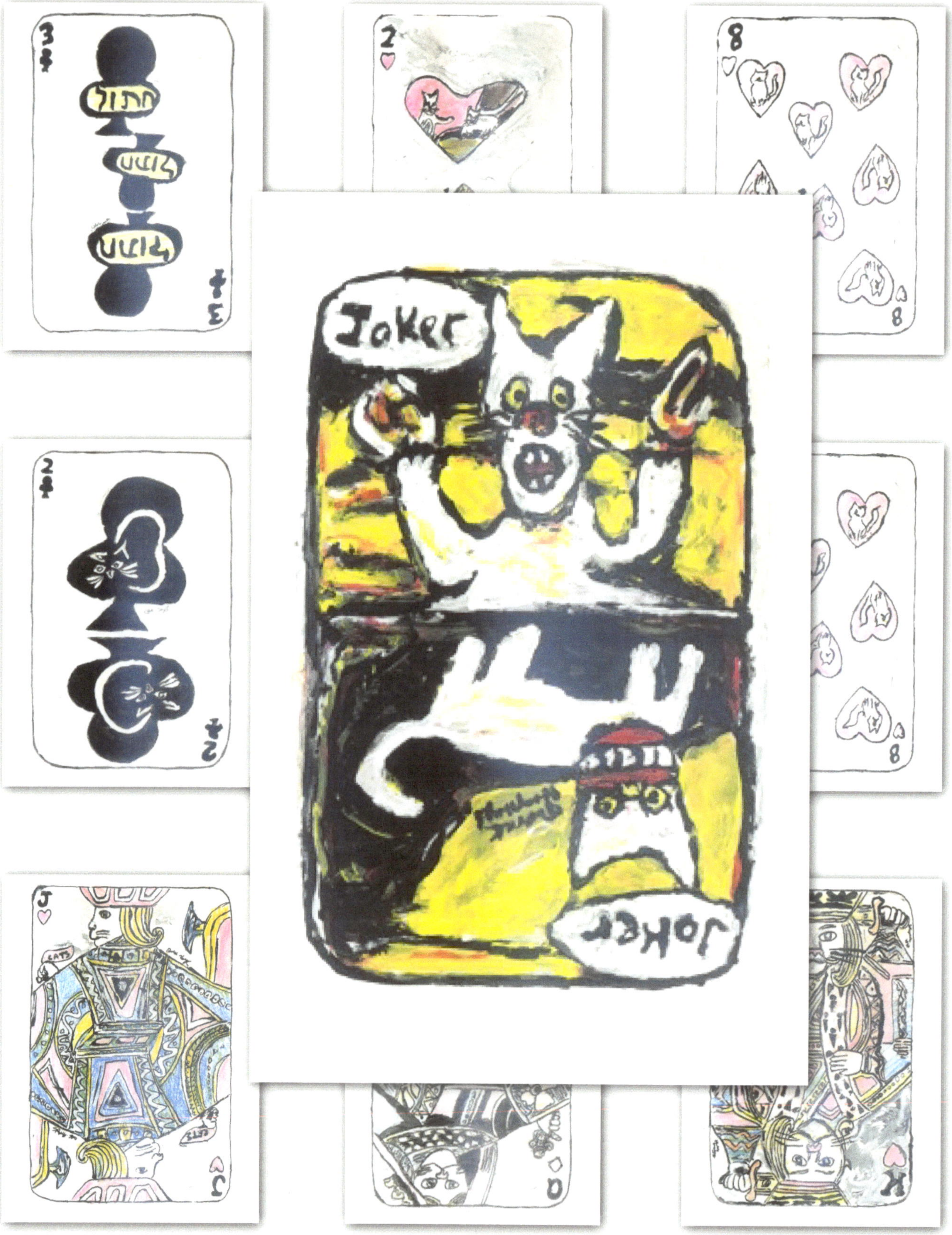
Joker
Joker

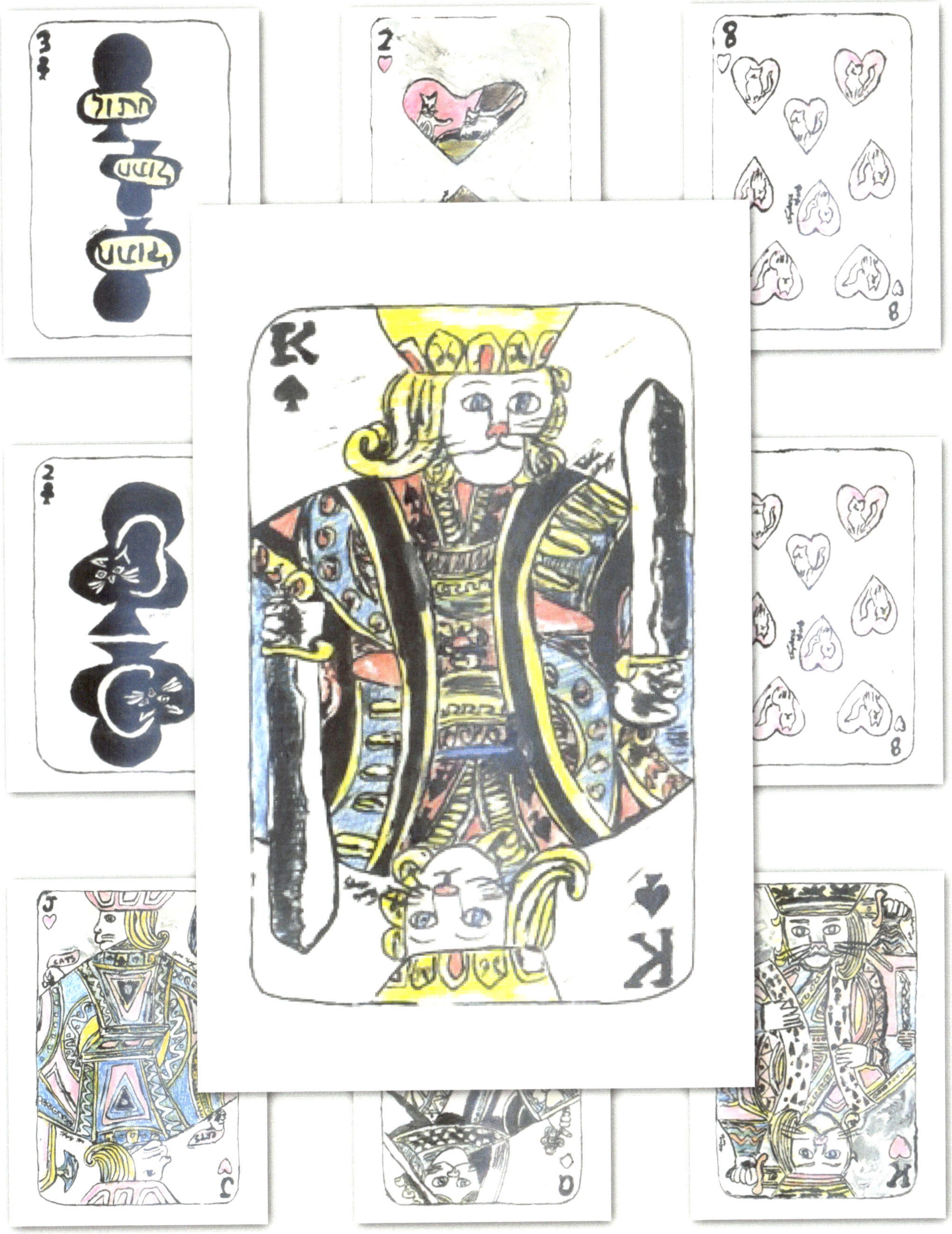

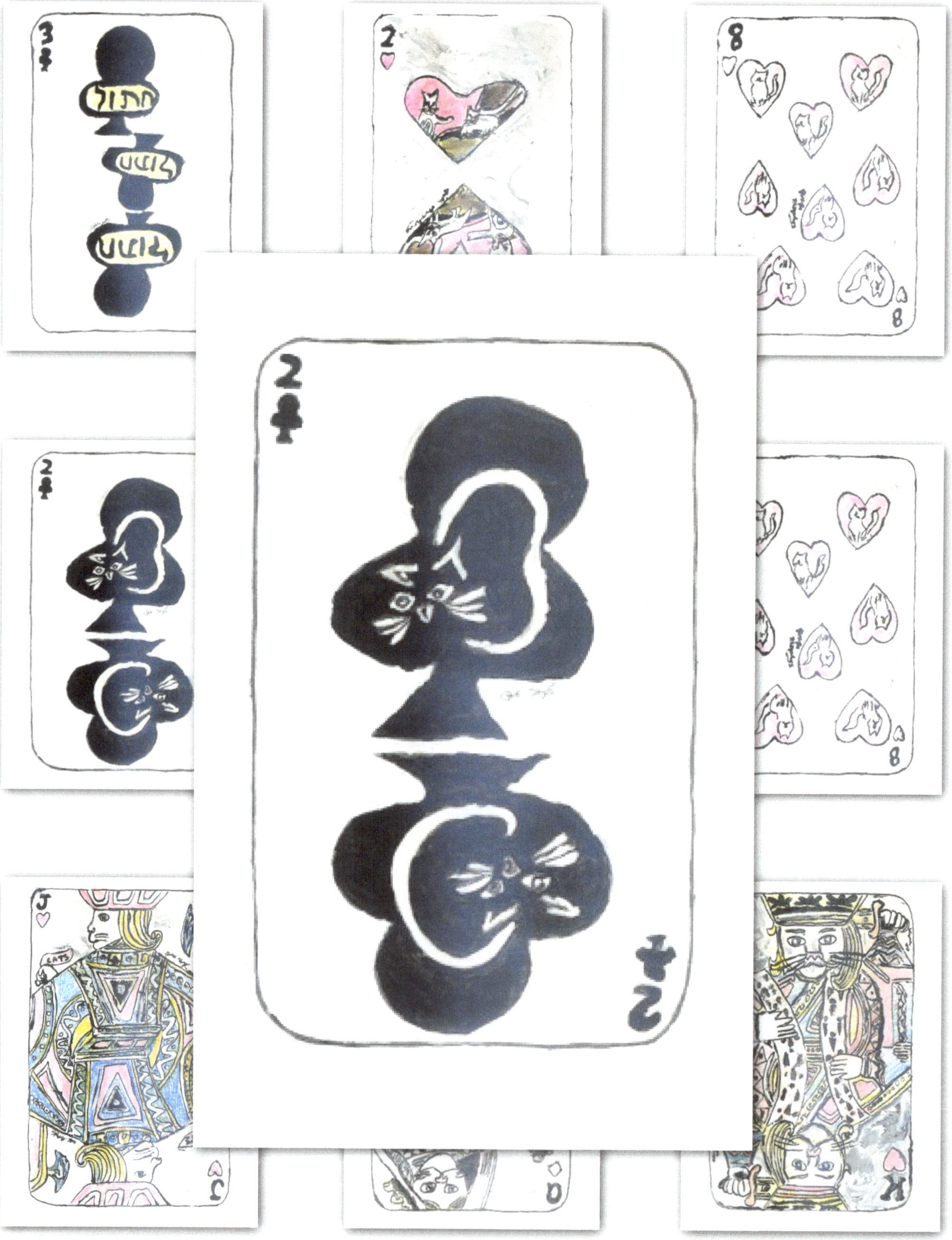

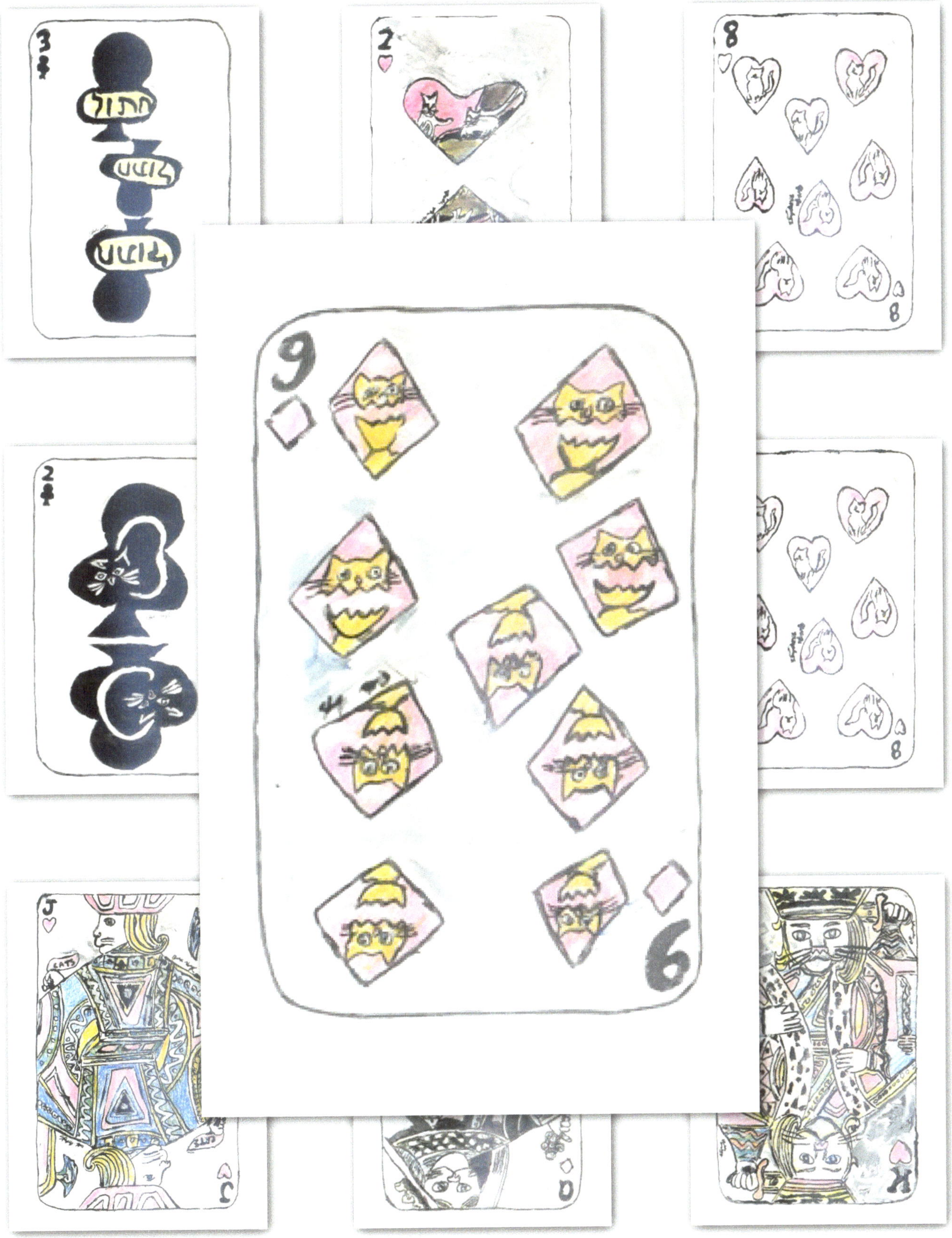
חתול

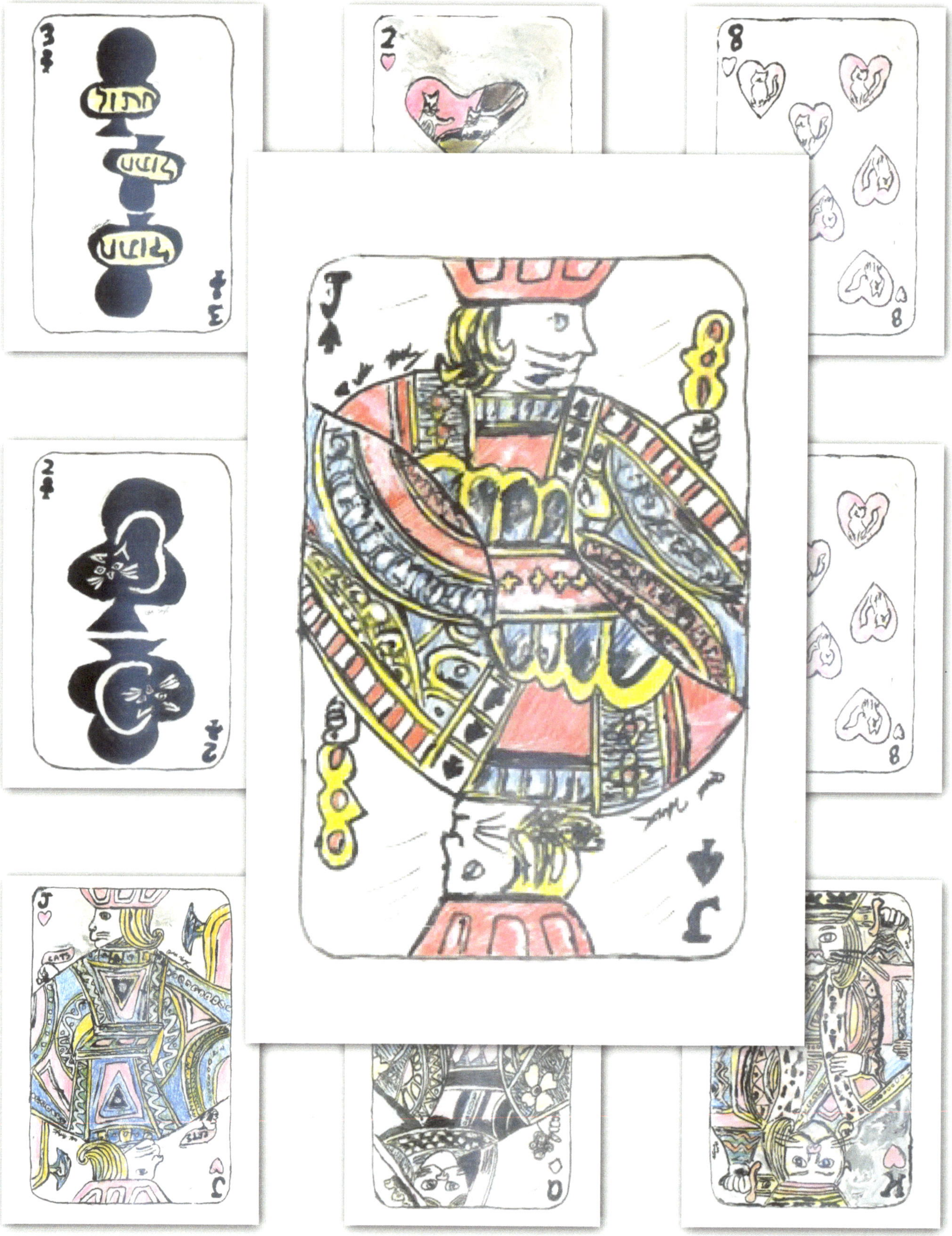

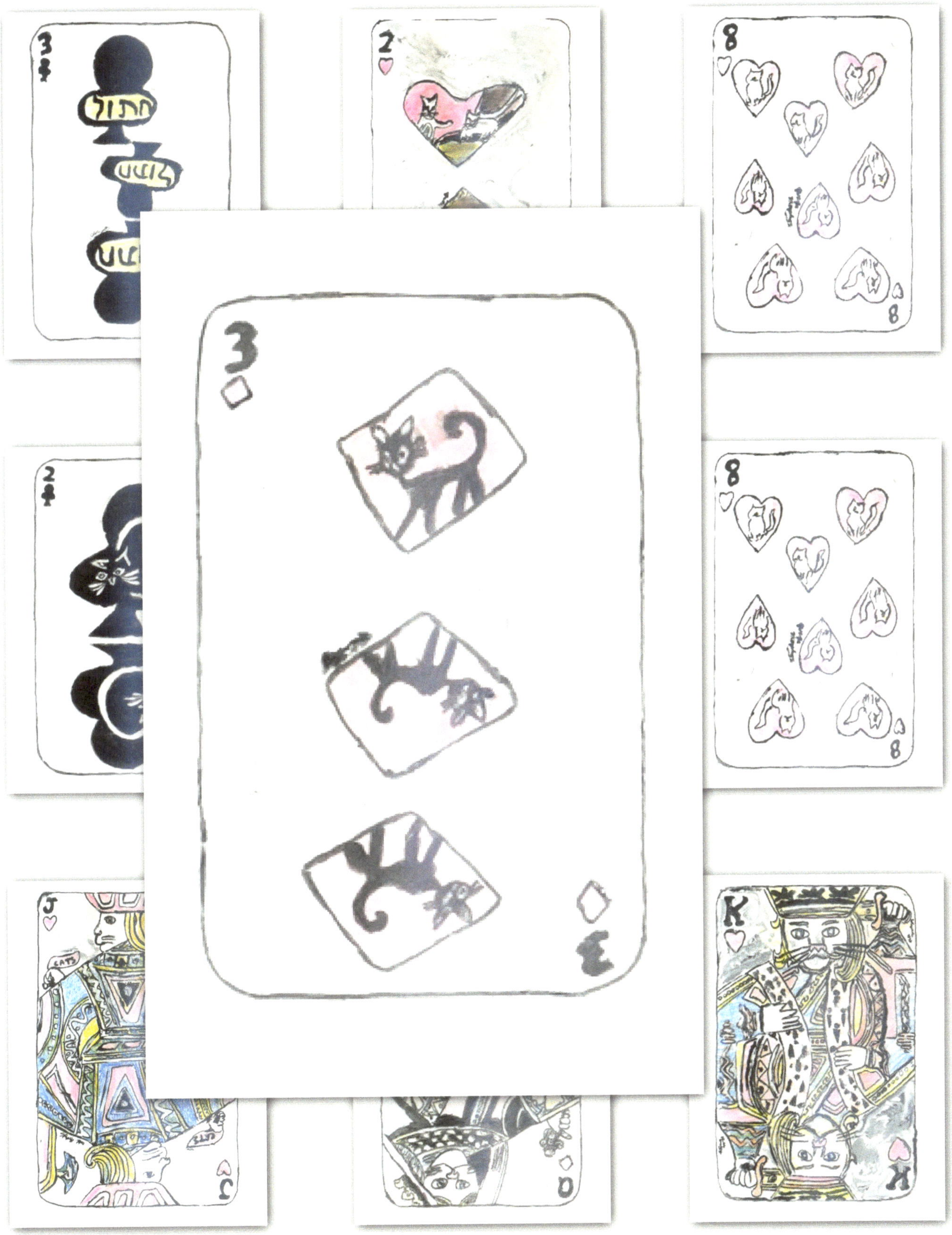

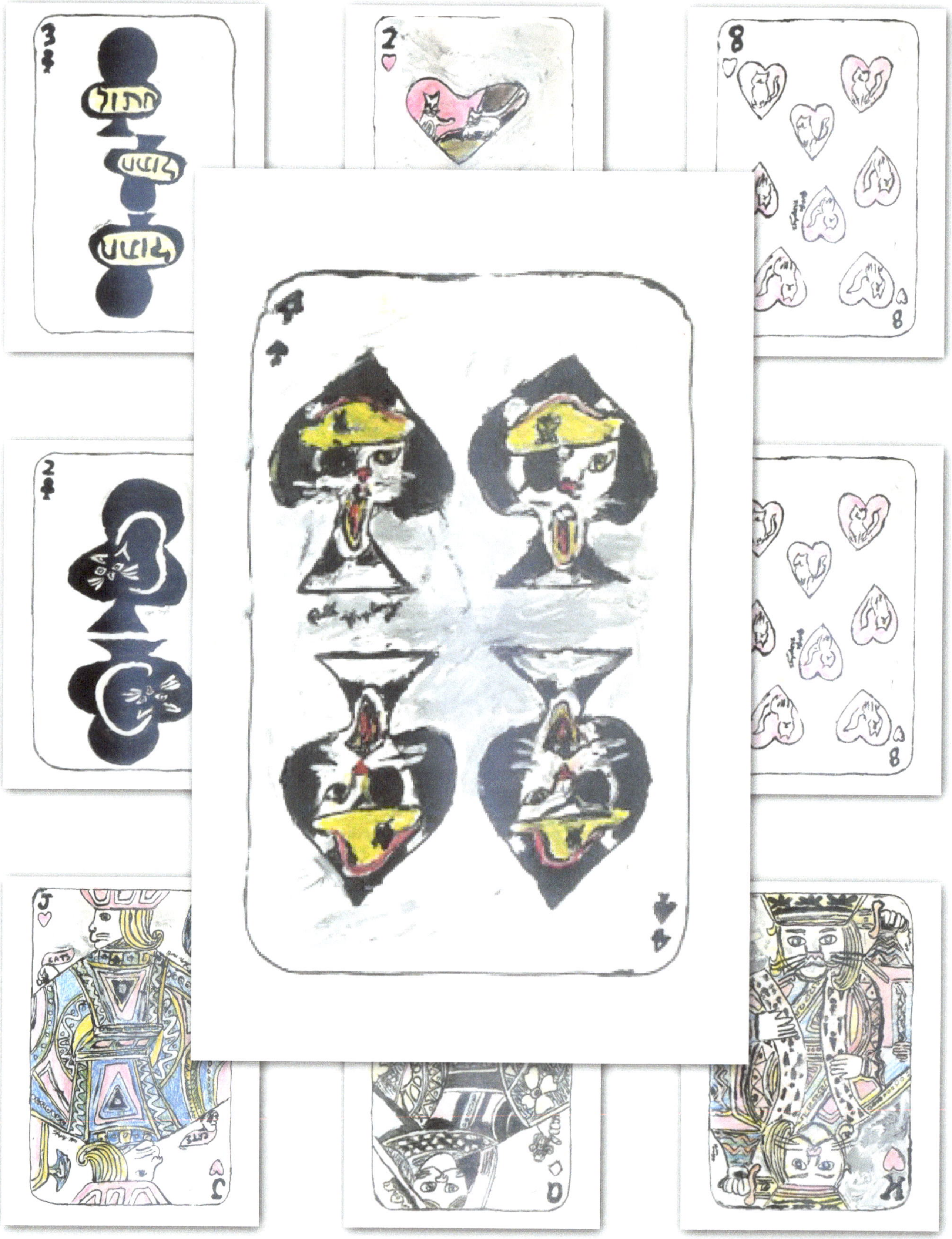

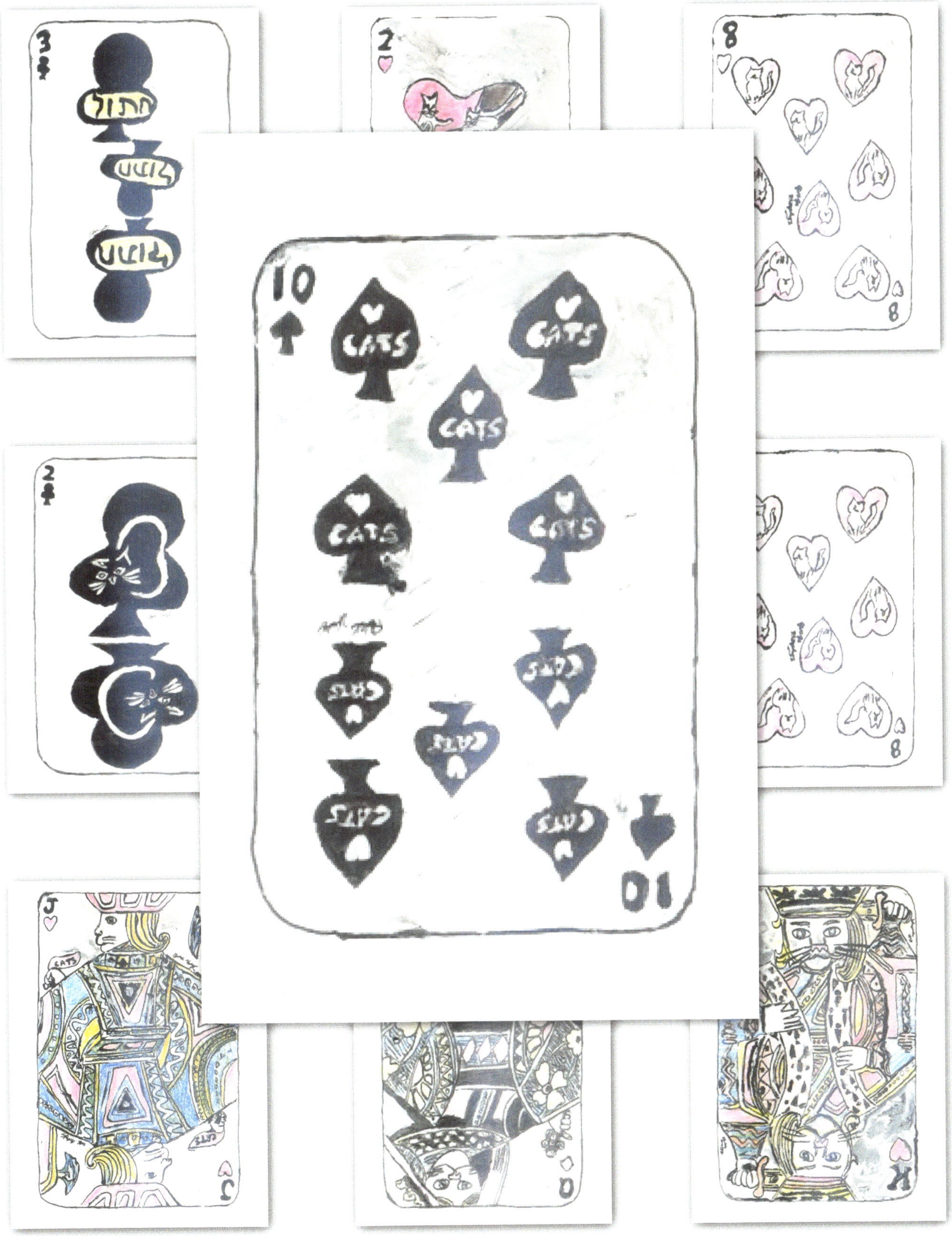
10
CATS

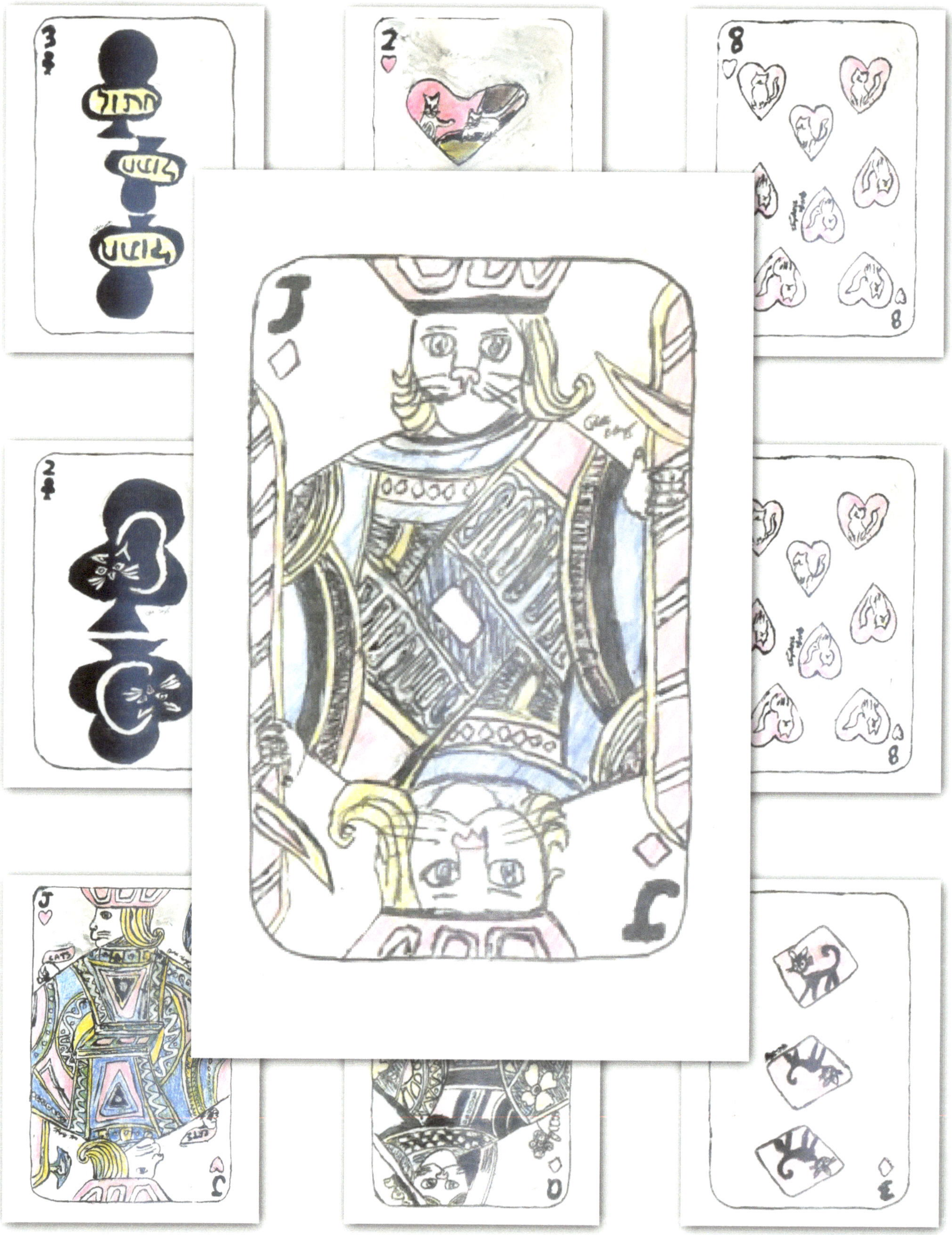

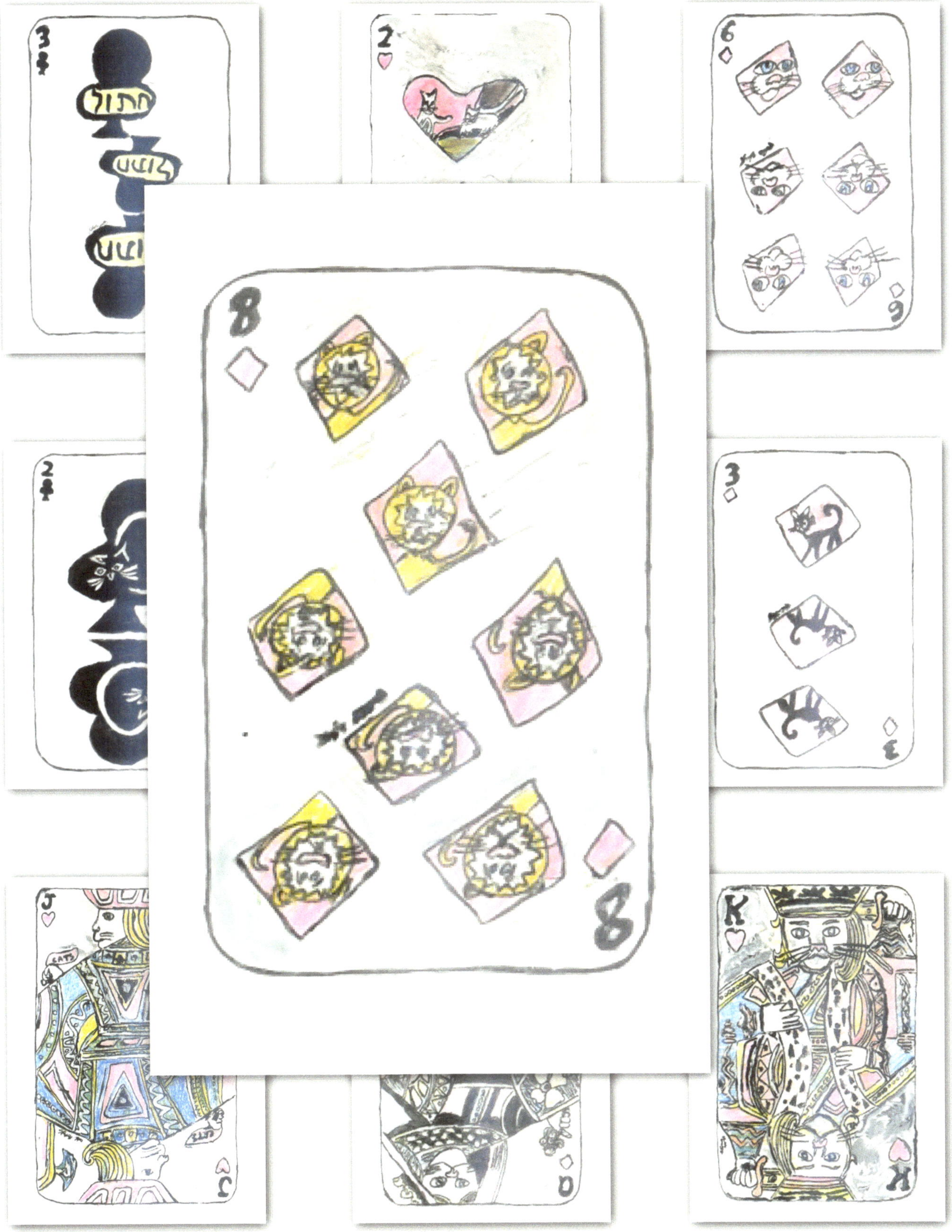

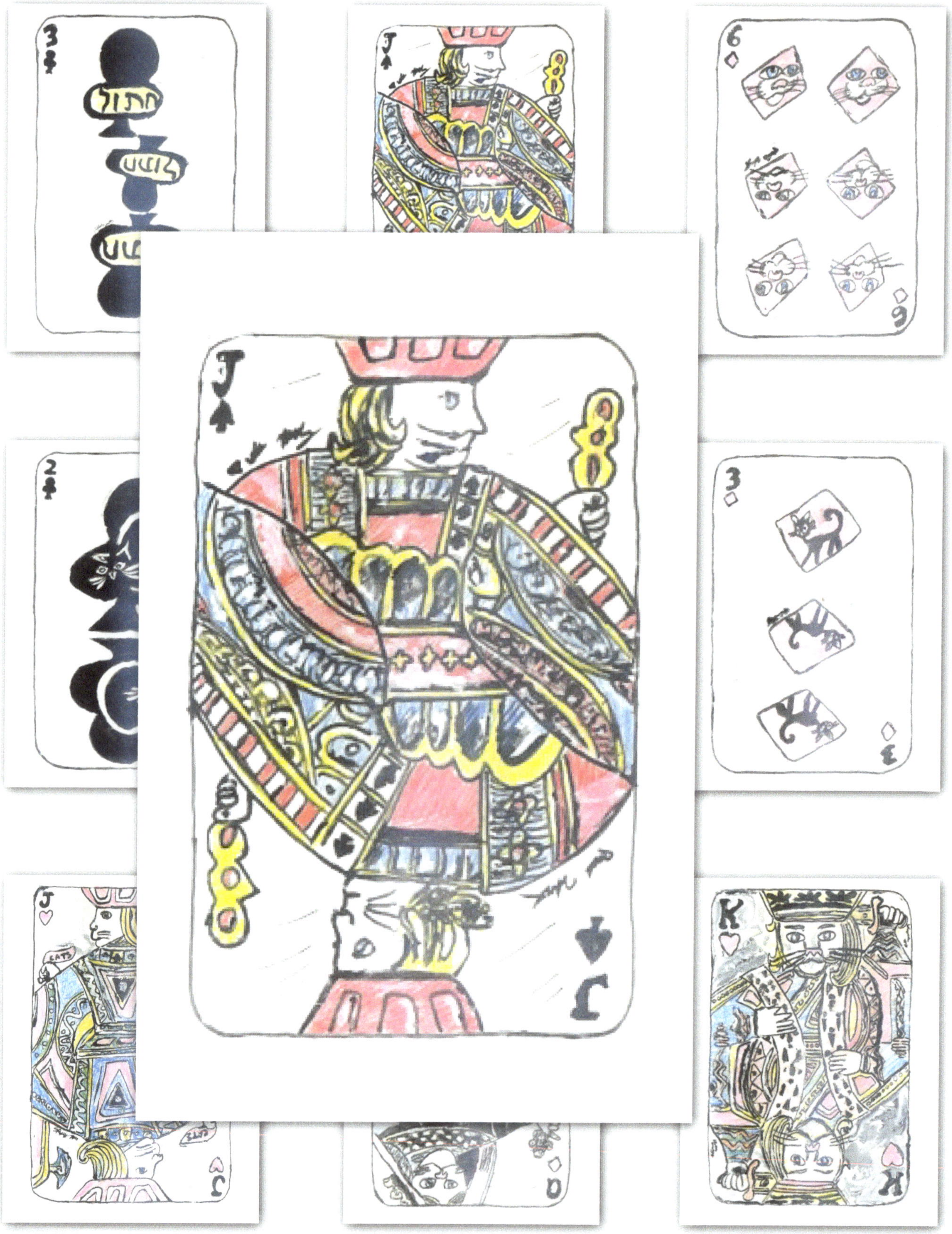

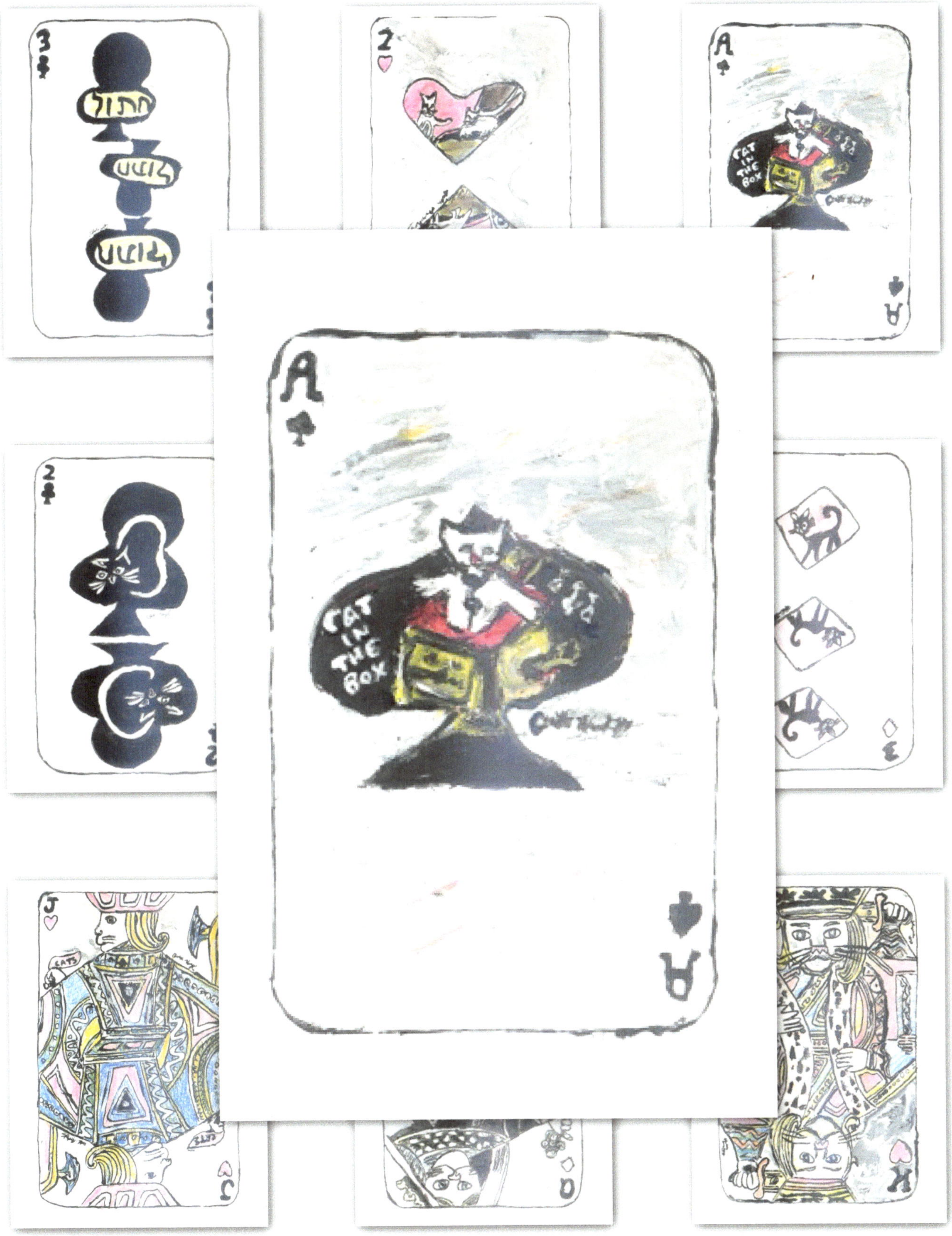
CAT
IN
THE
BOX

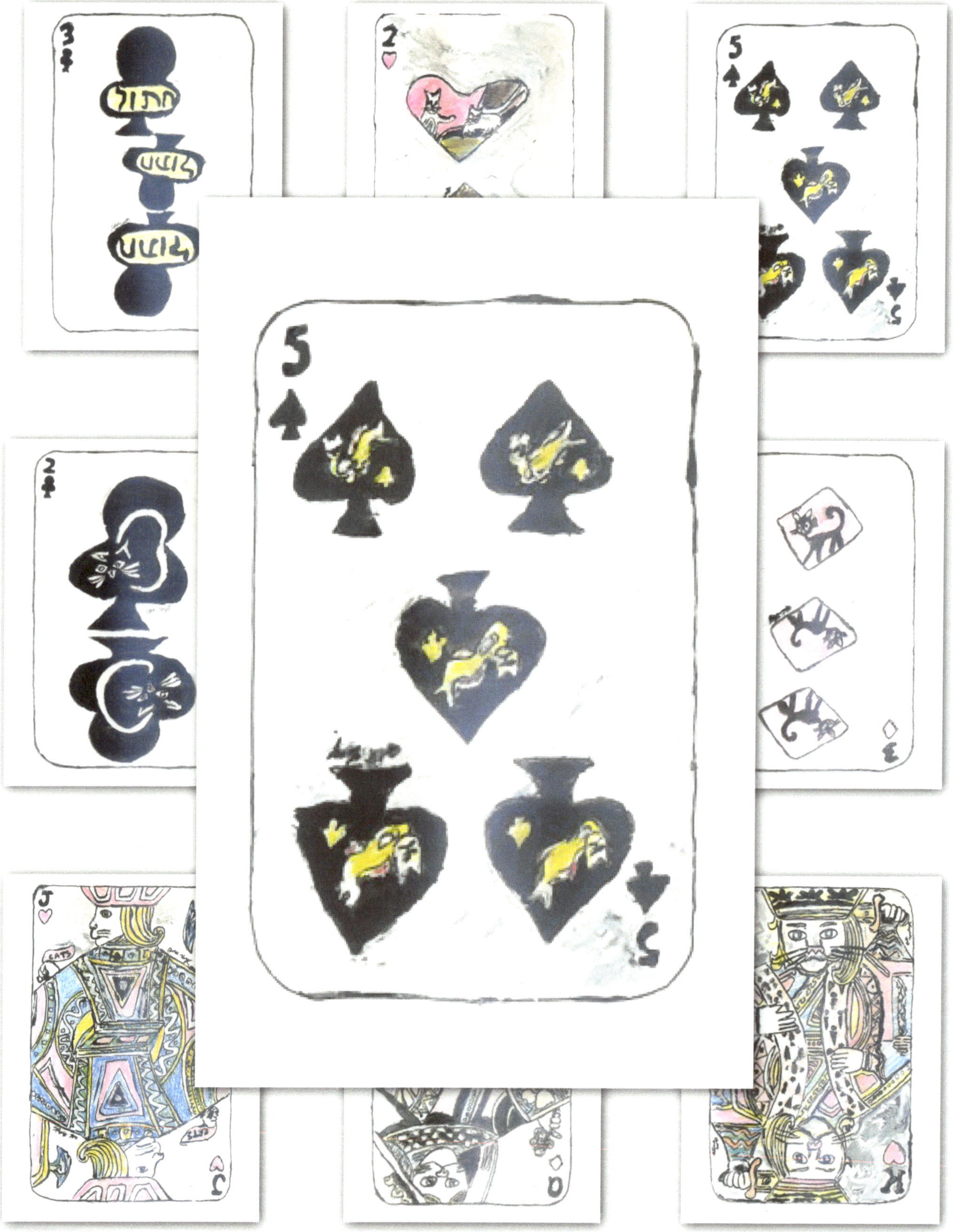

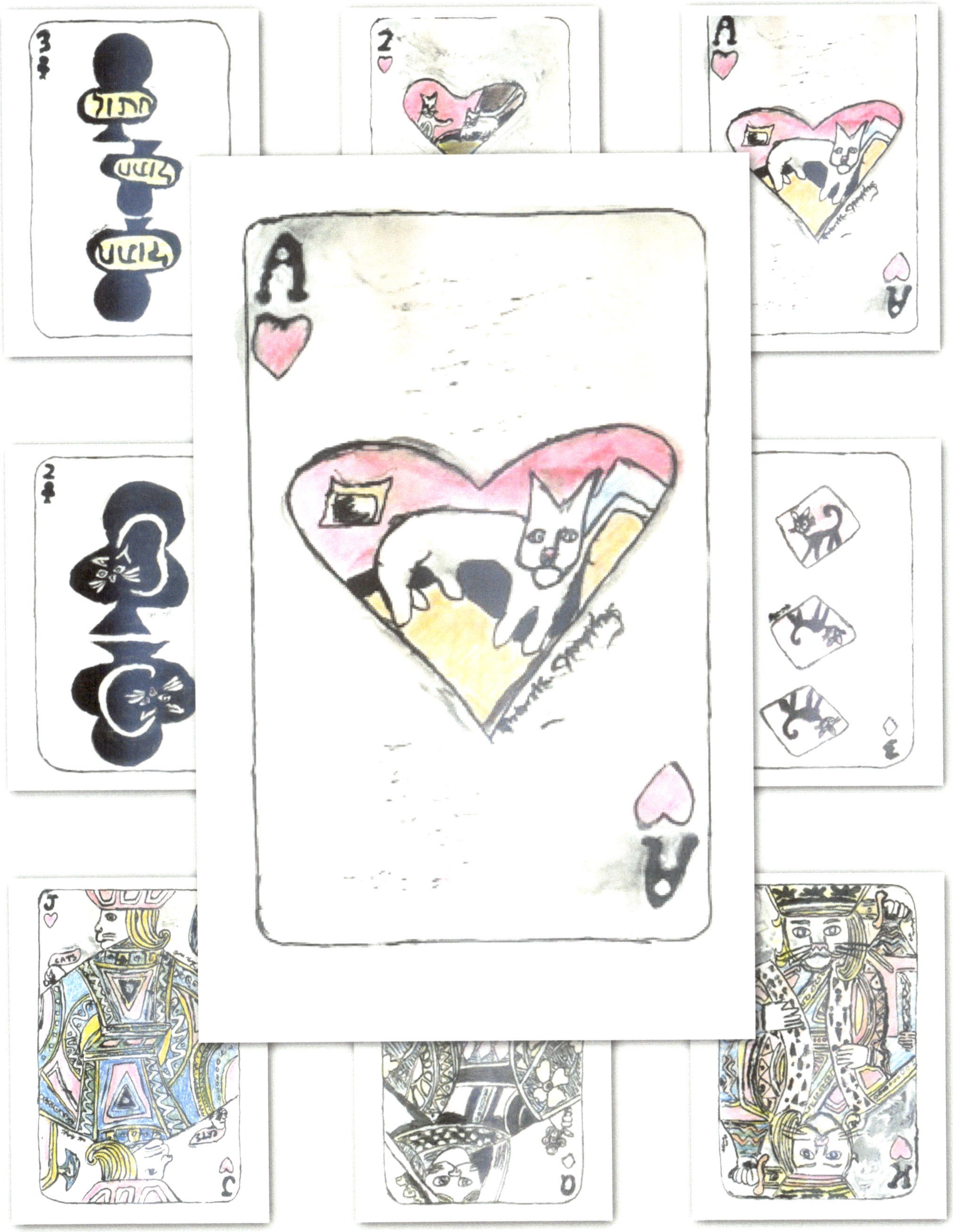

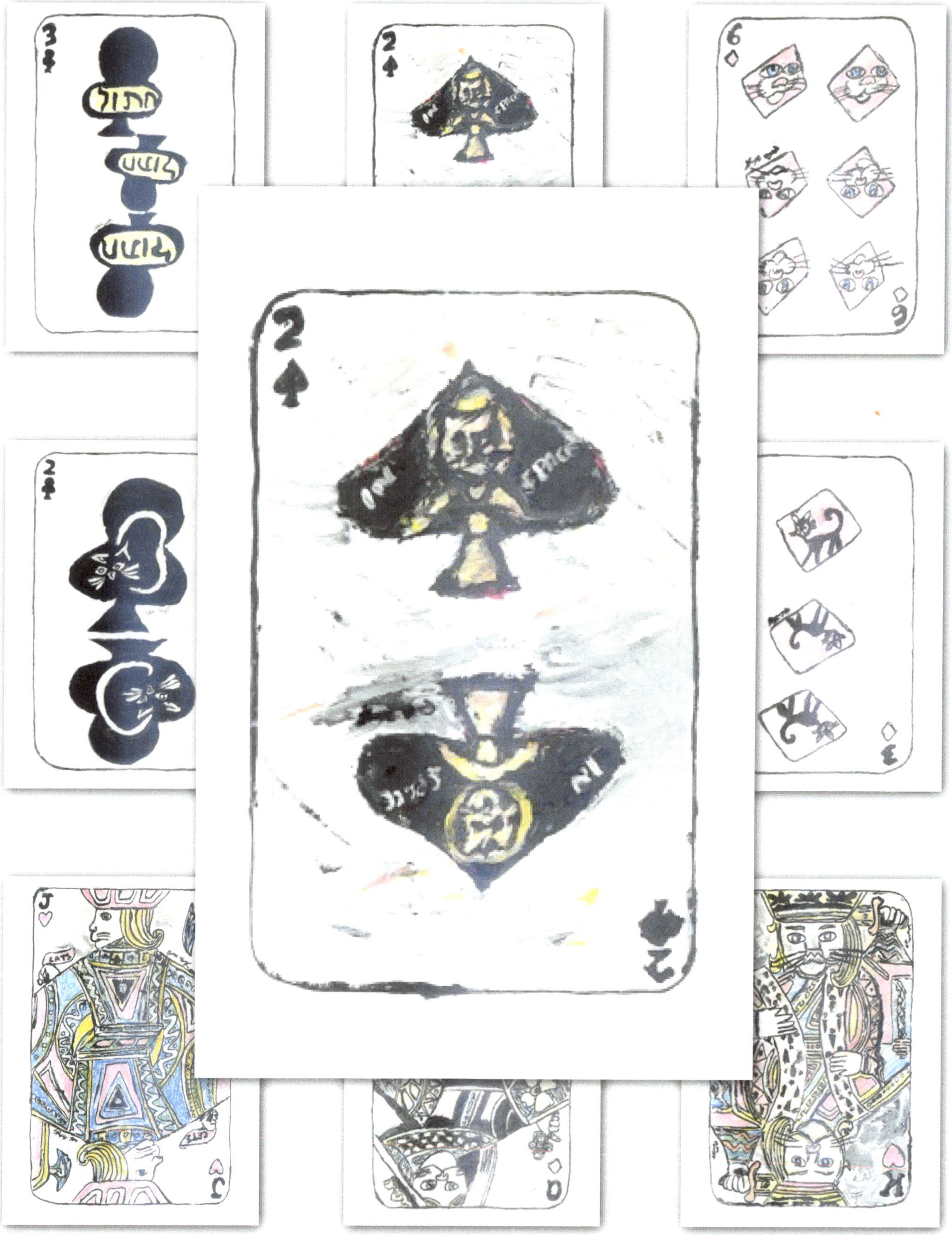

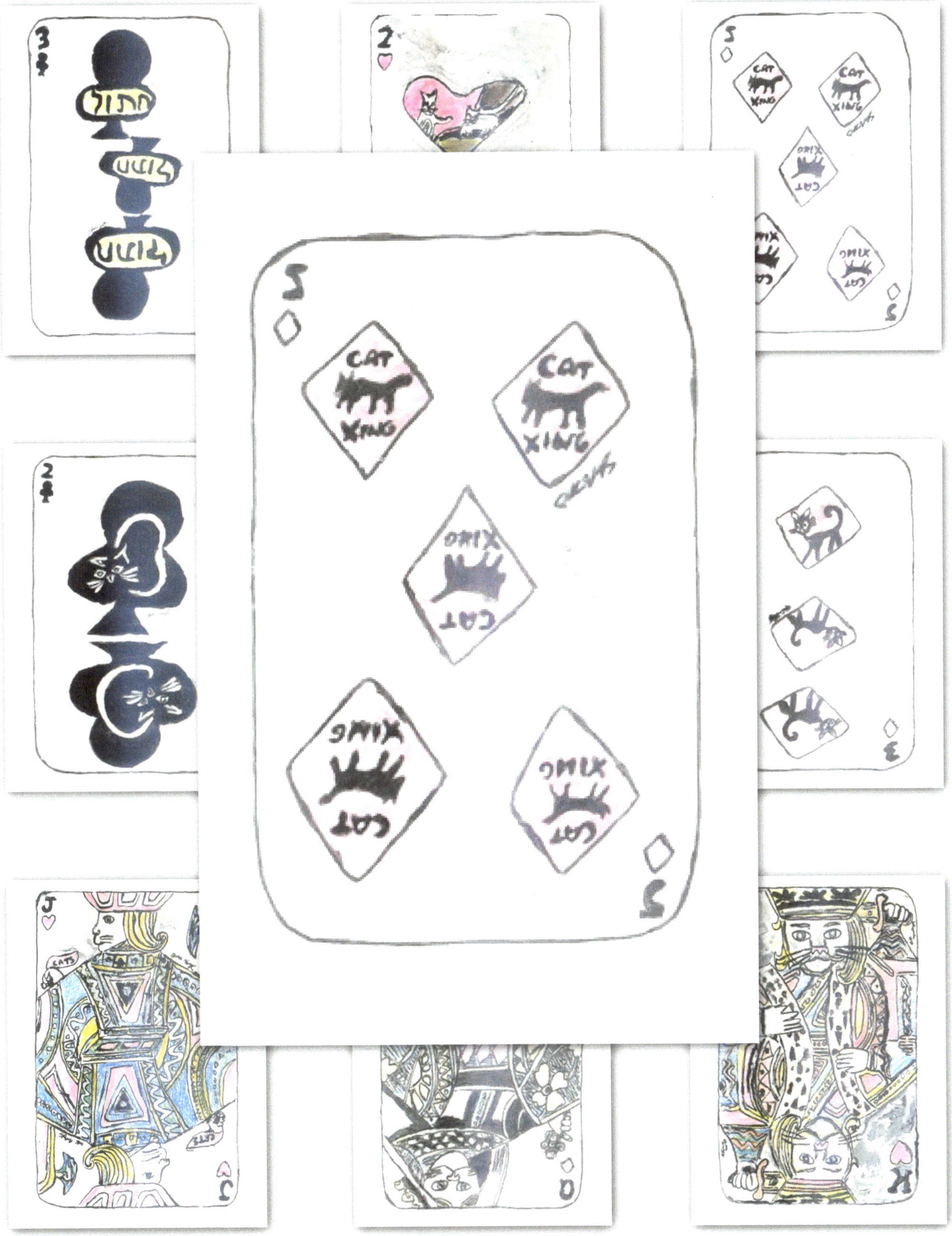
CAT
XING

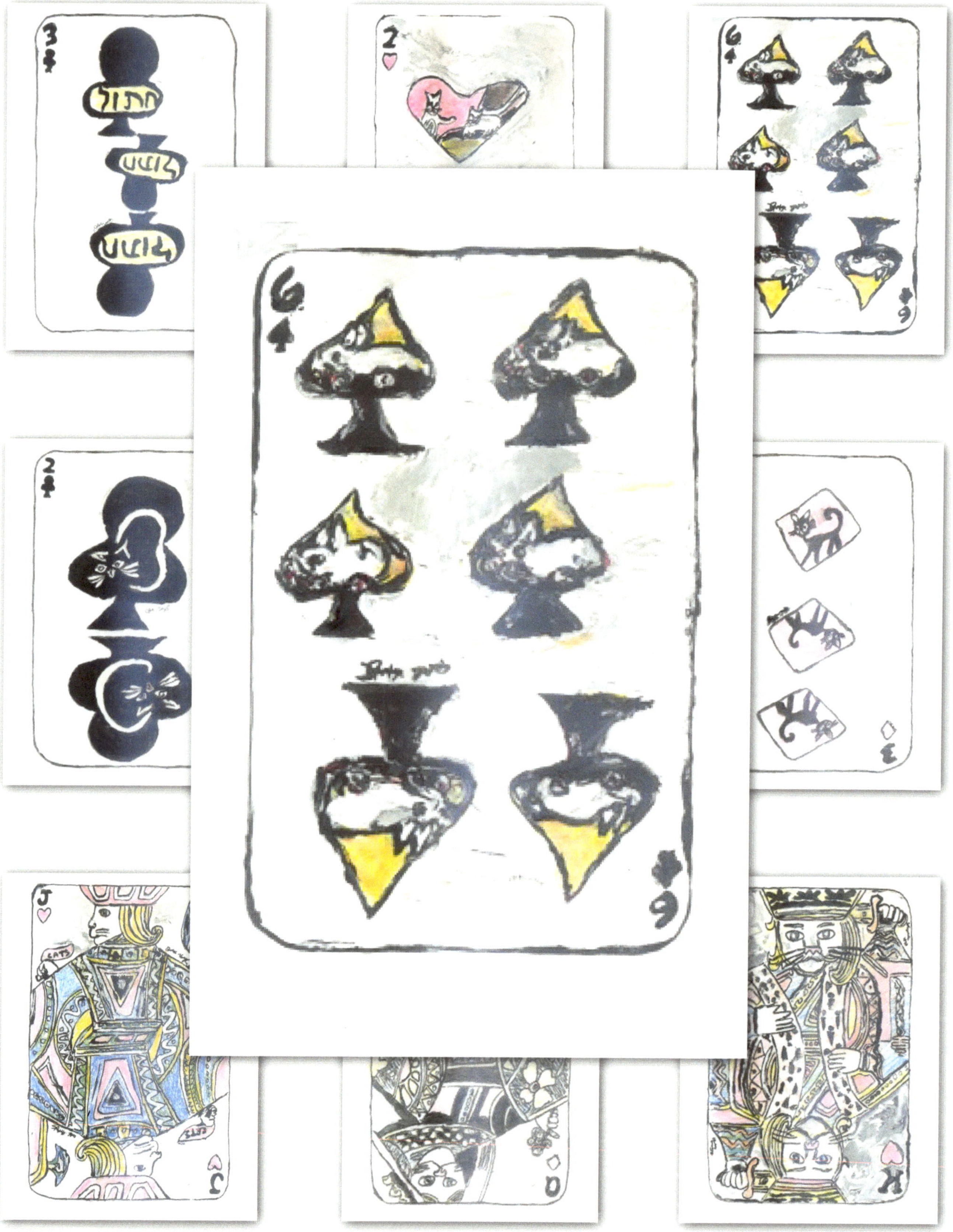
חתול

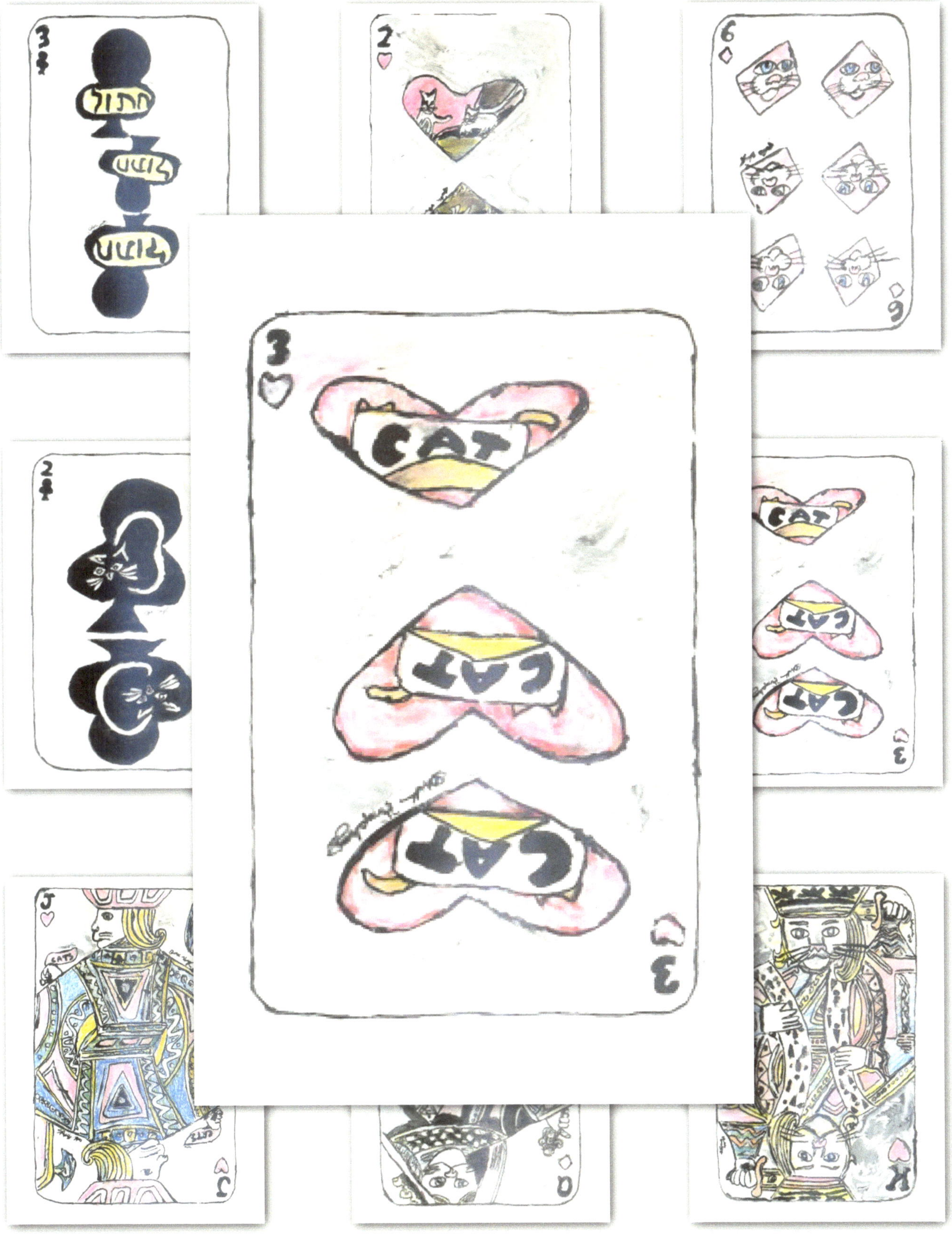
חתול
CAT

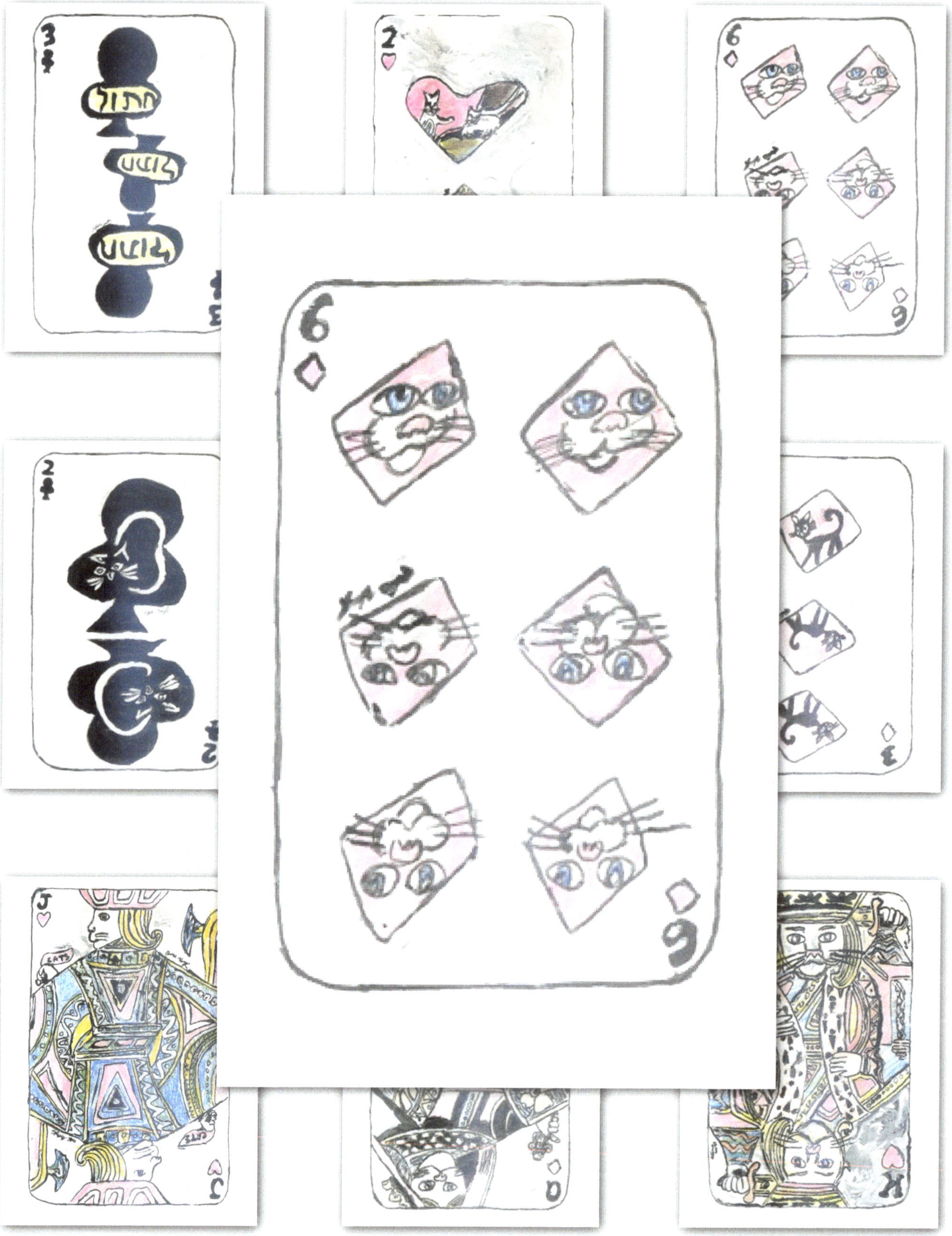

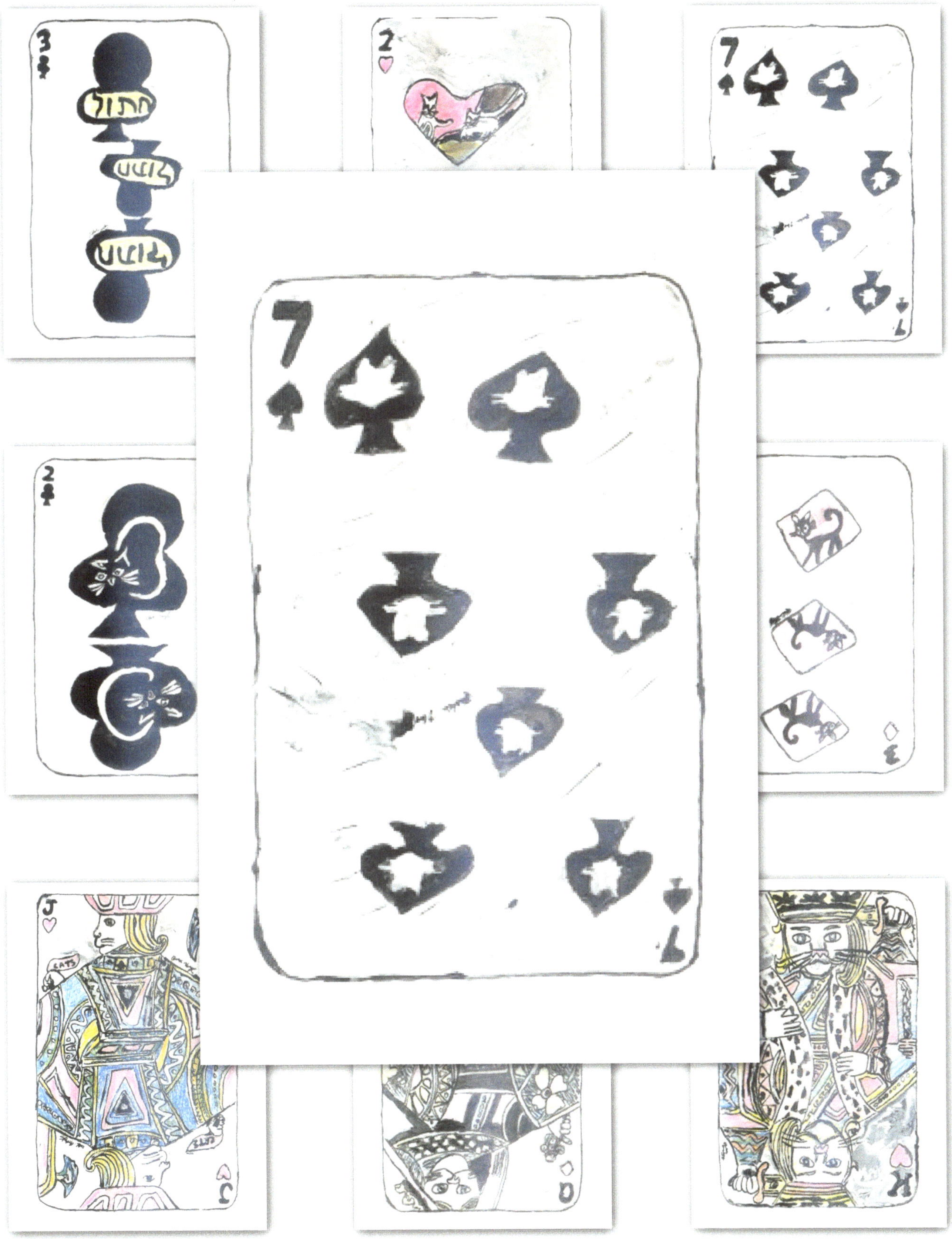

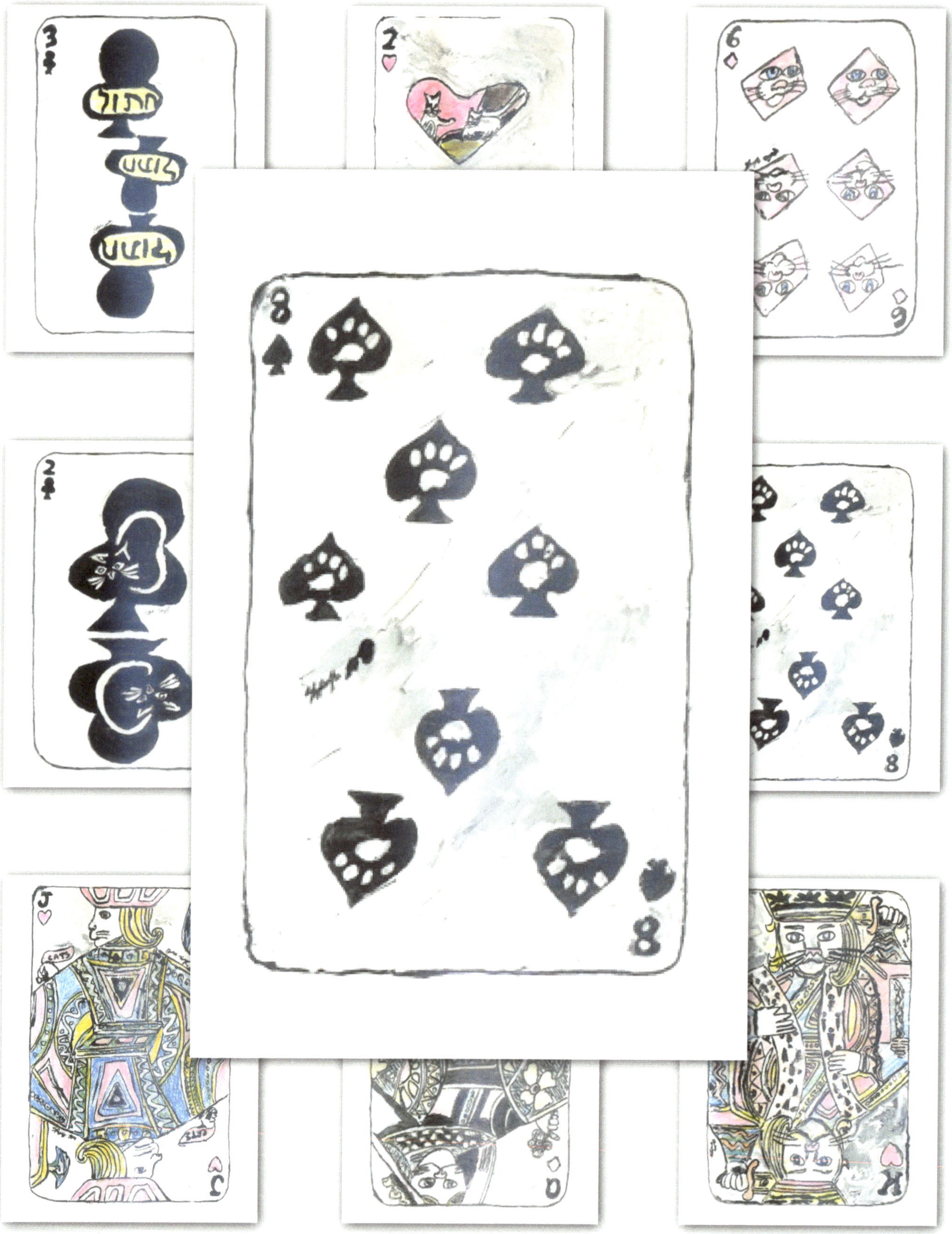

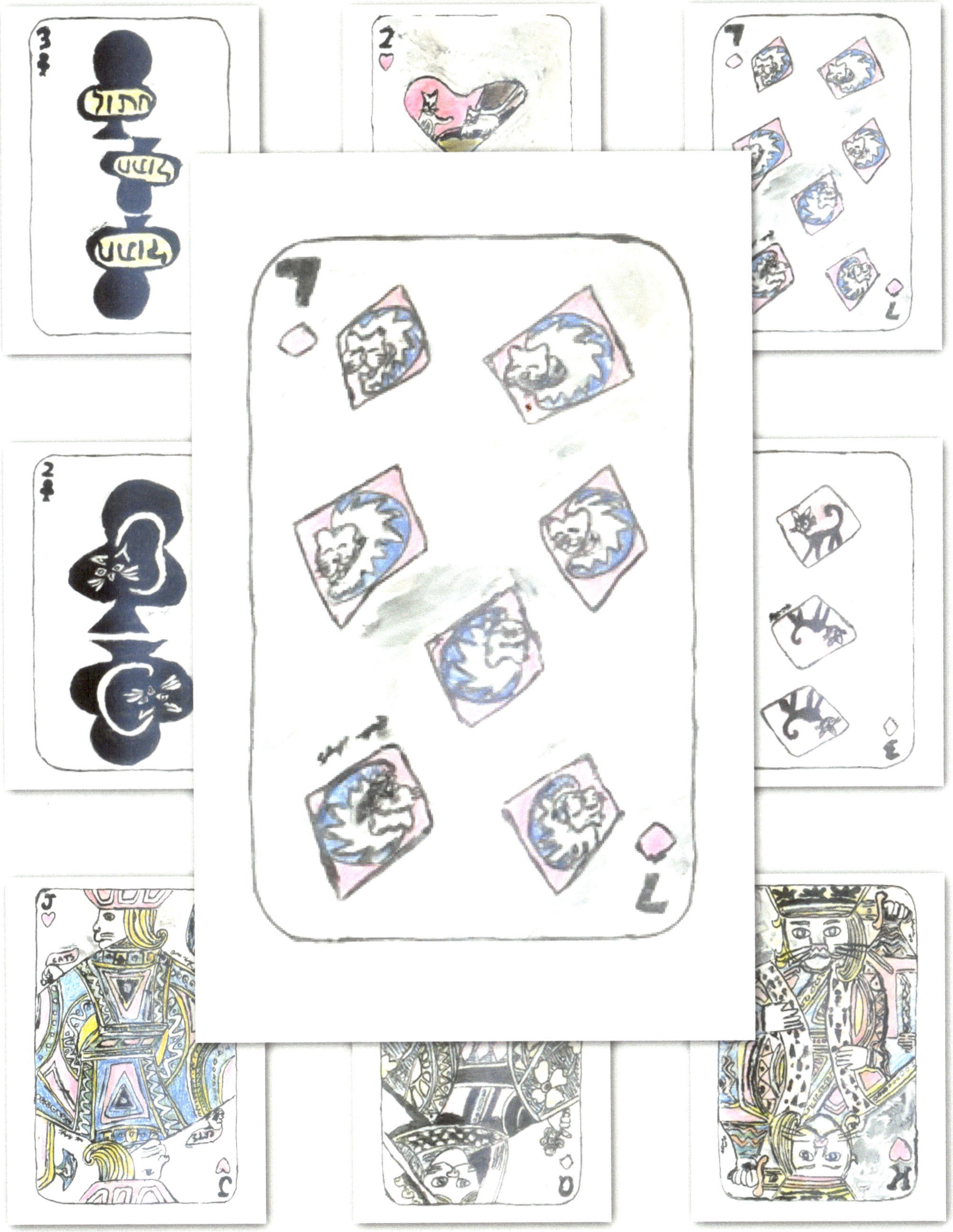

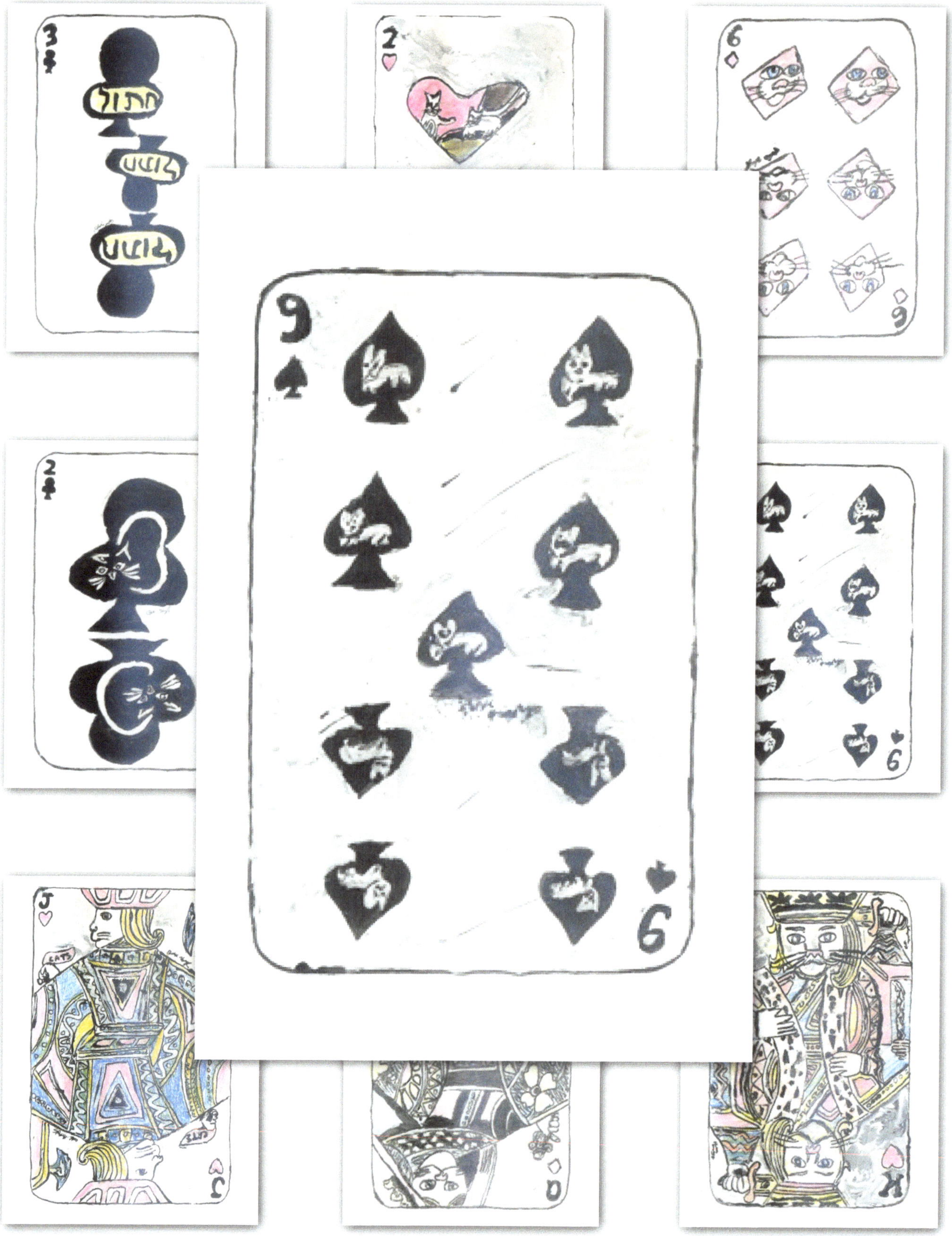
חתול
CATS

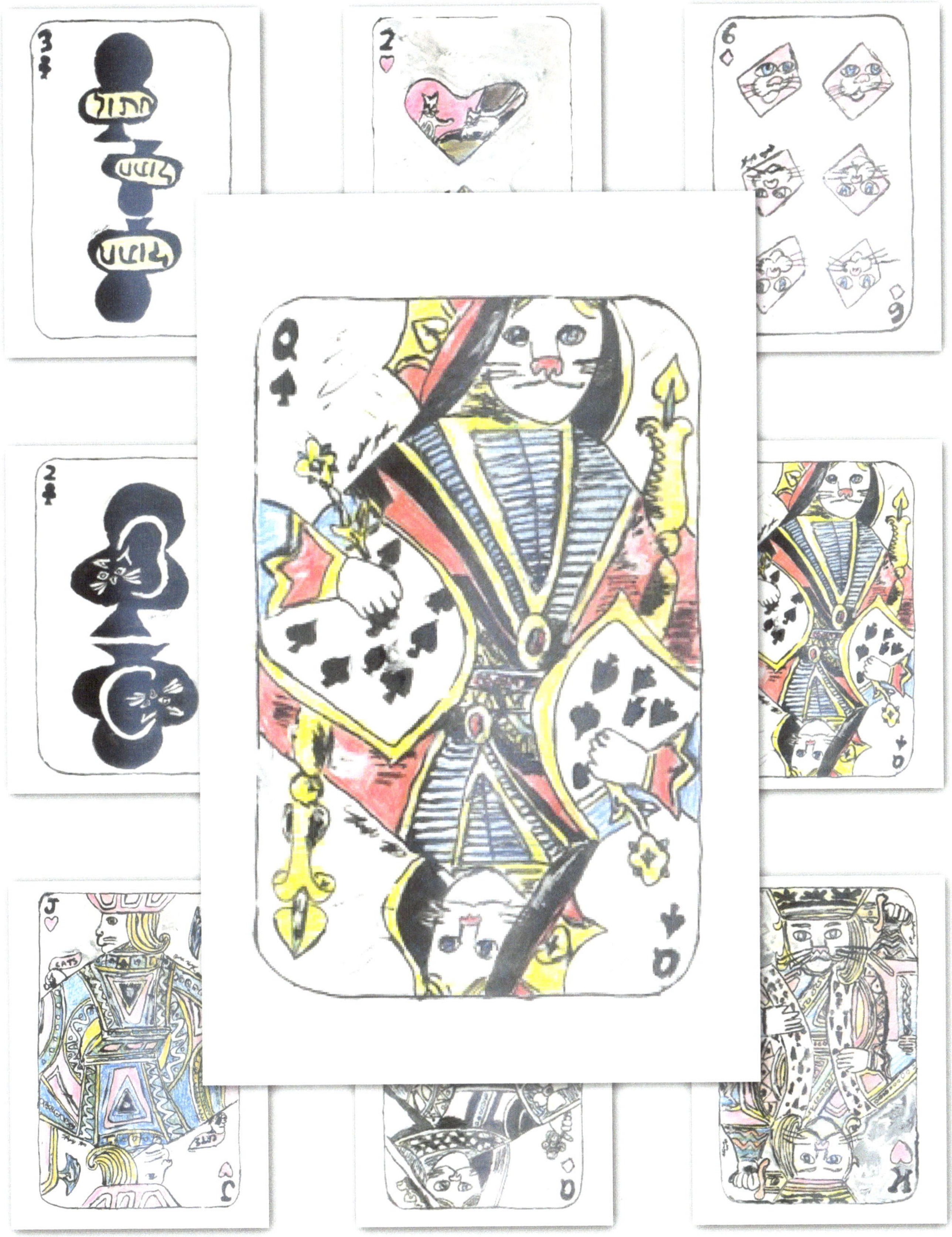

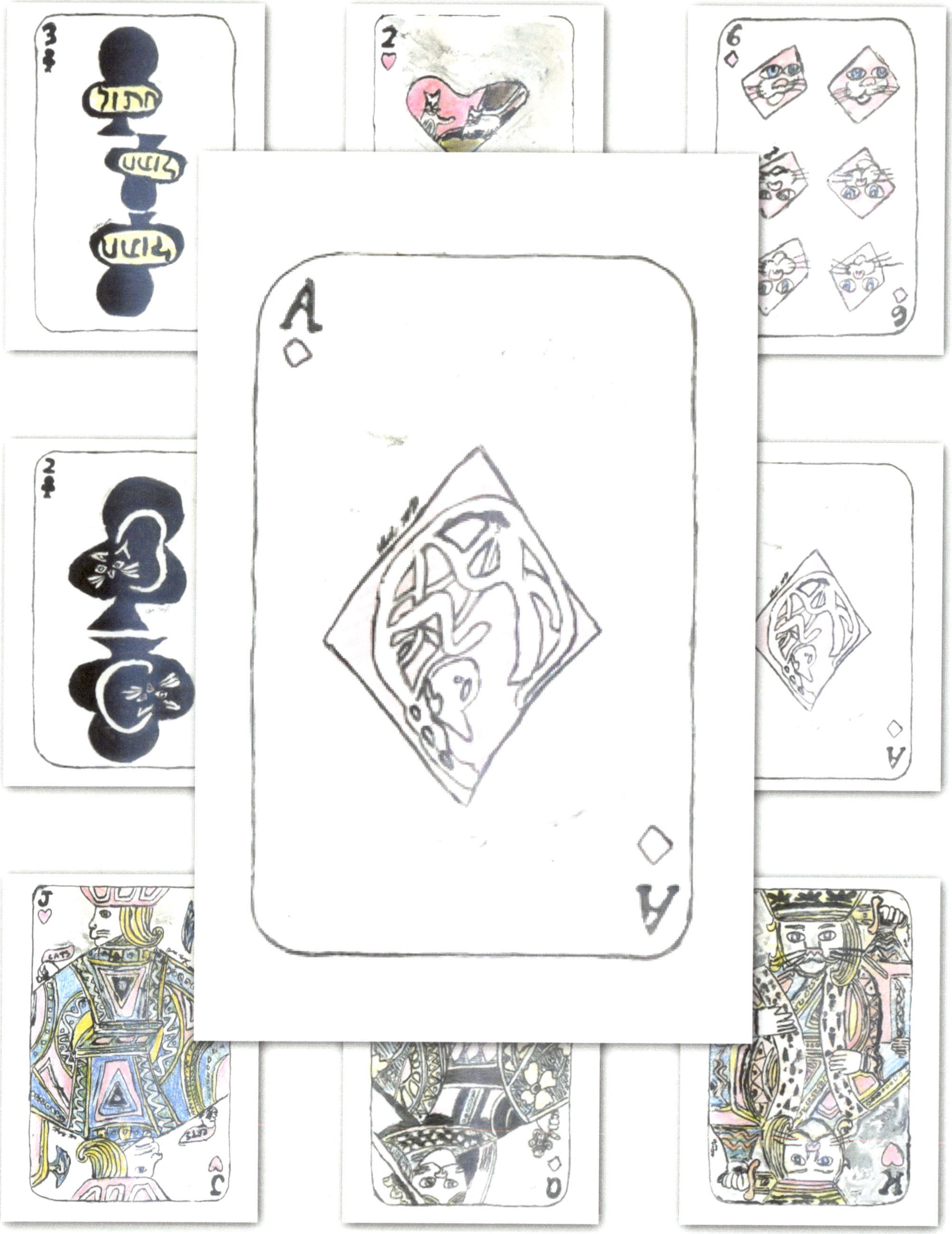

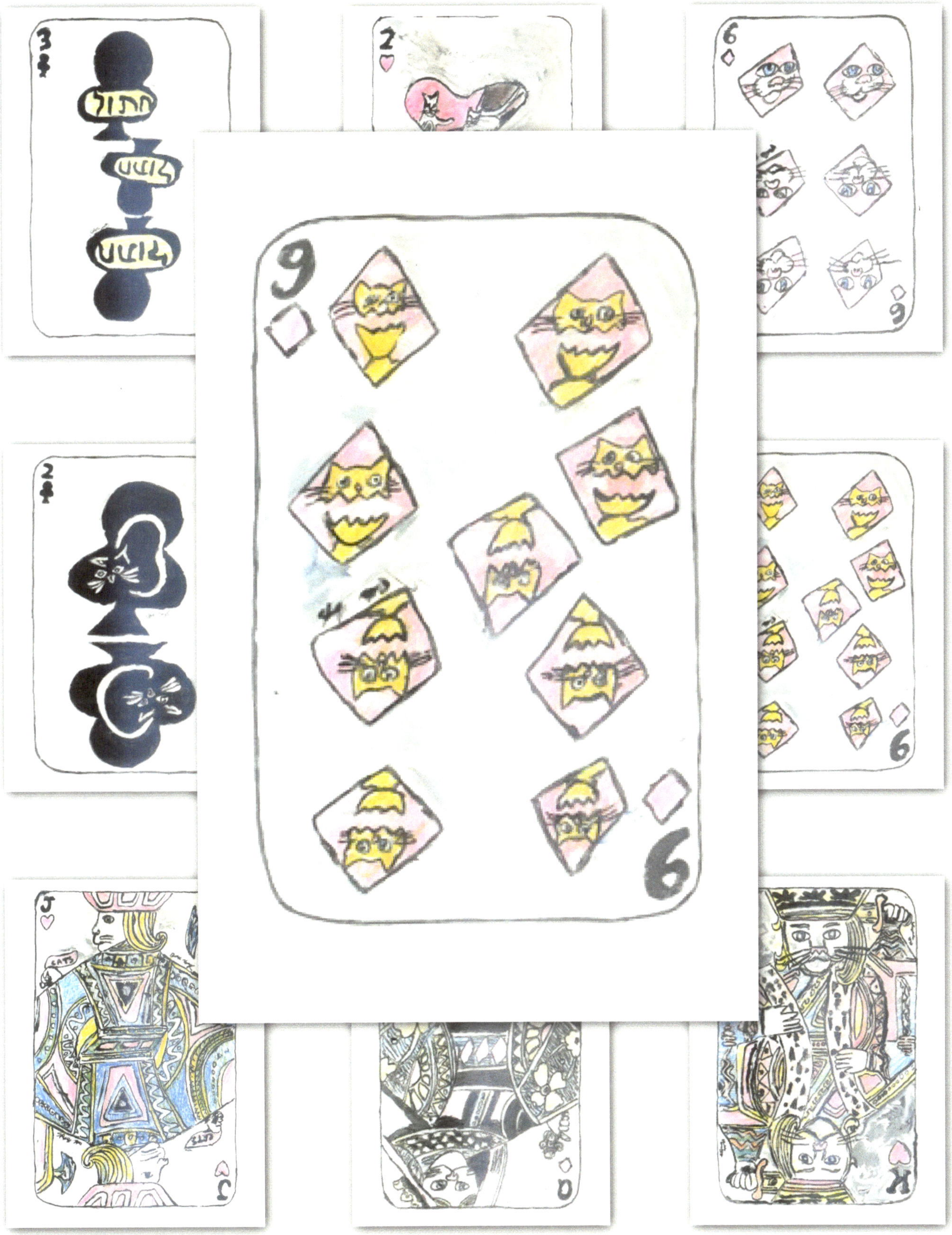

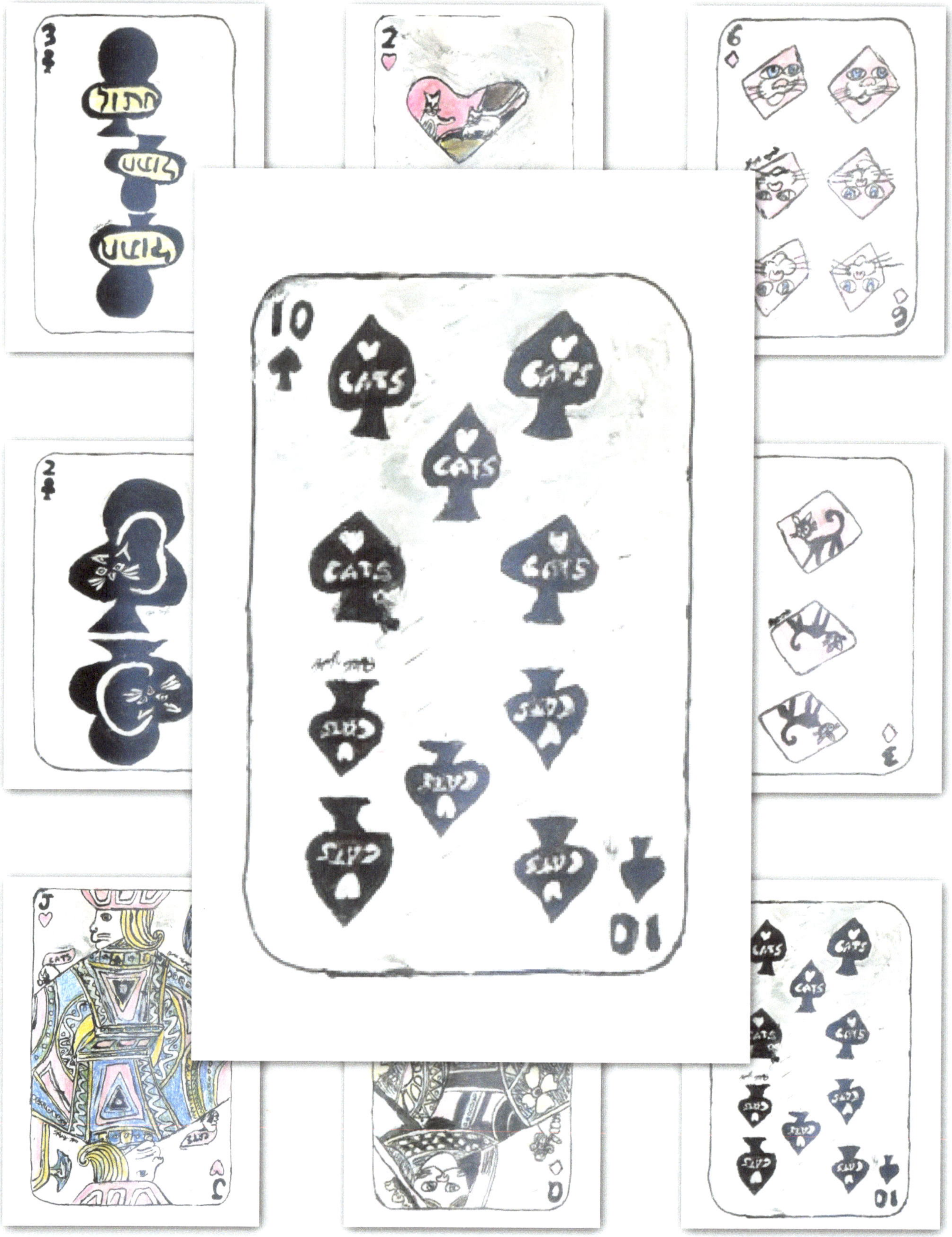
10
CATS

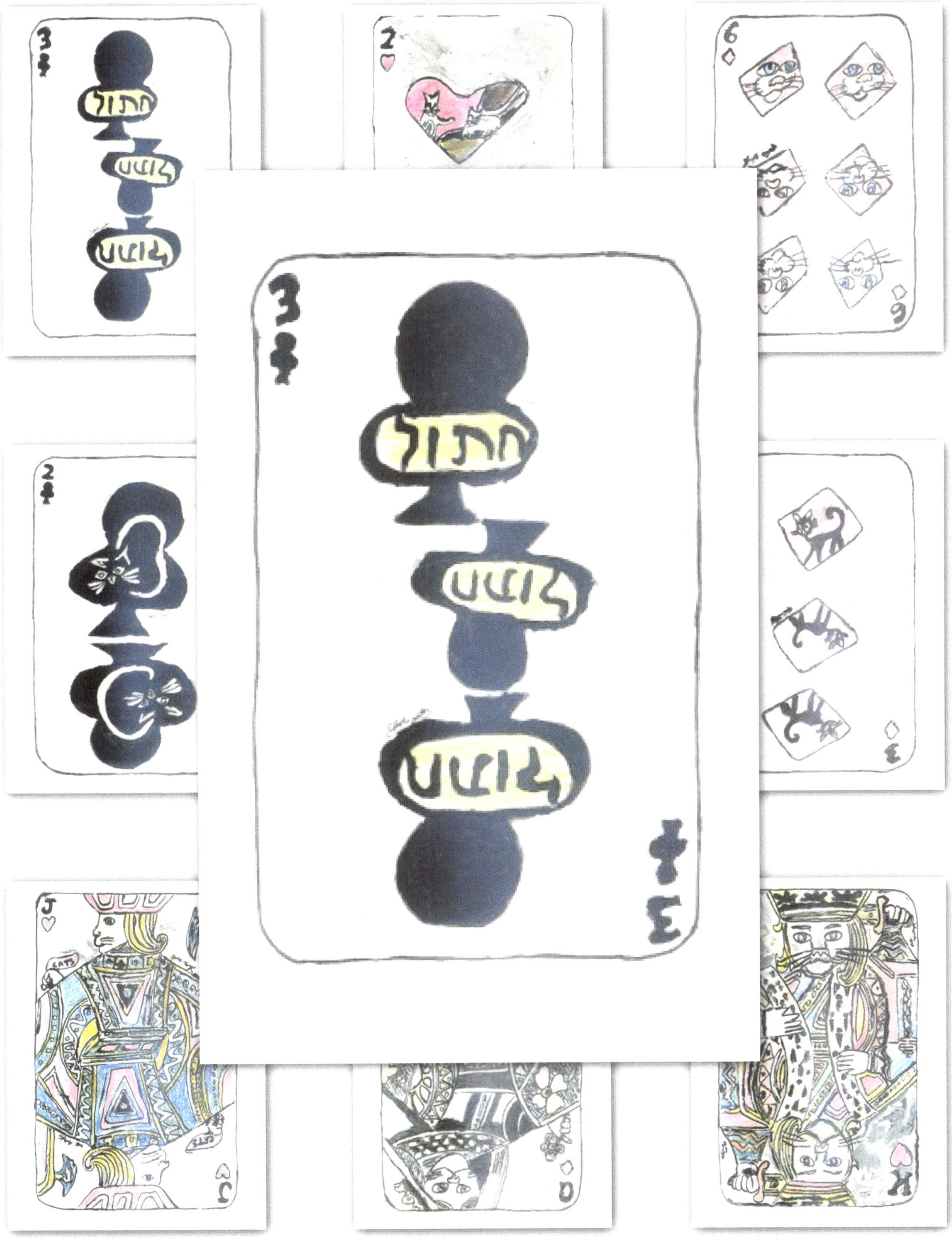
חתול

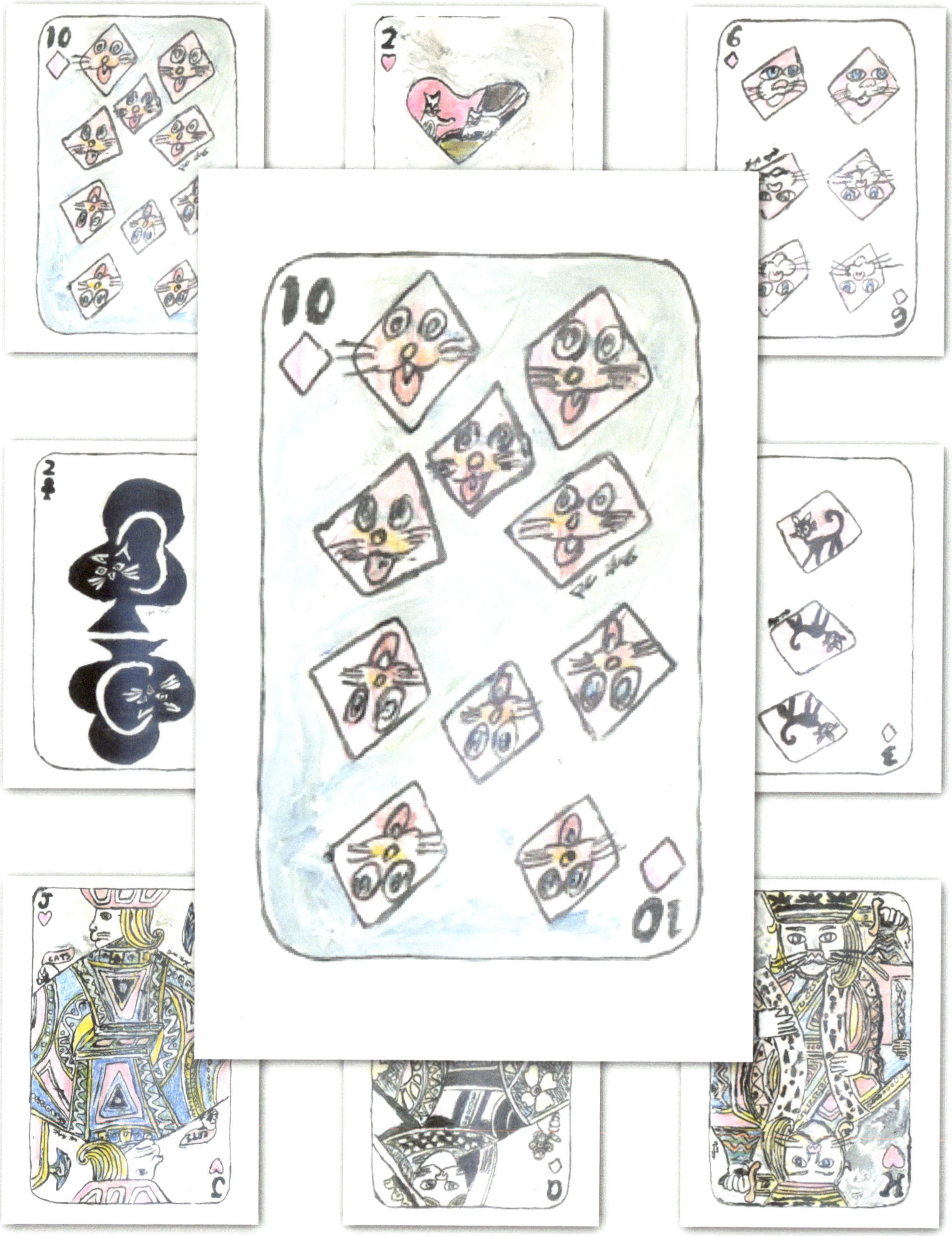

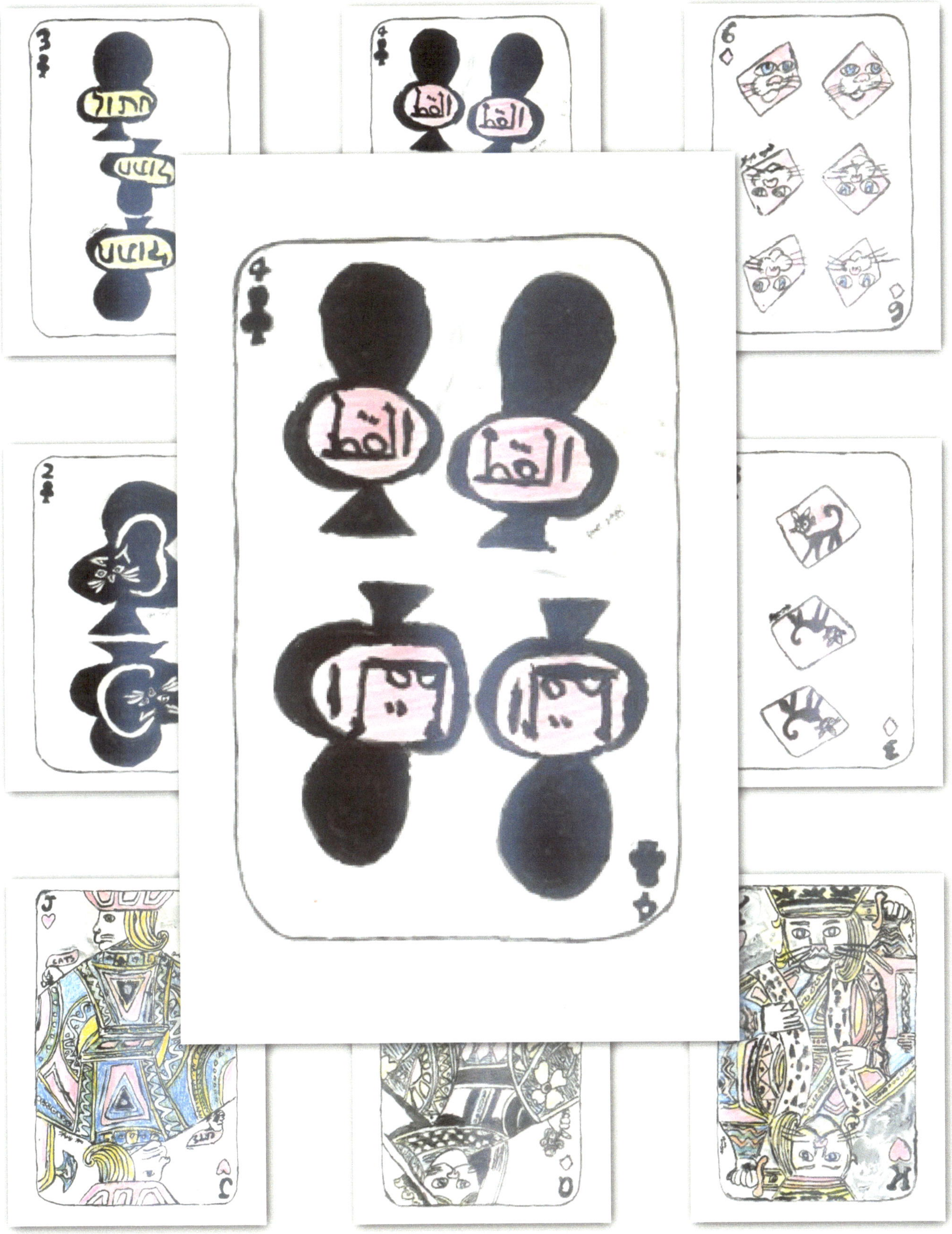
חתול
القط
القط

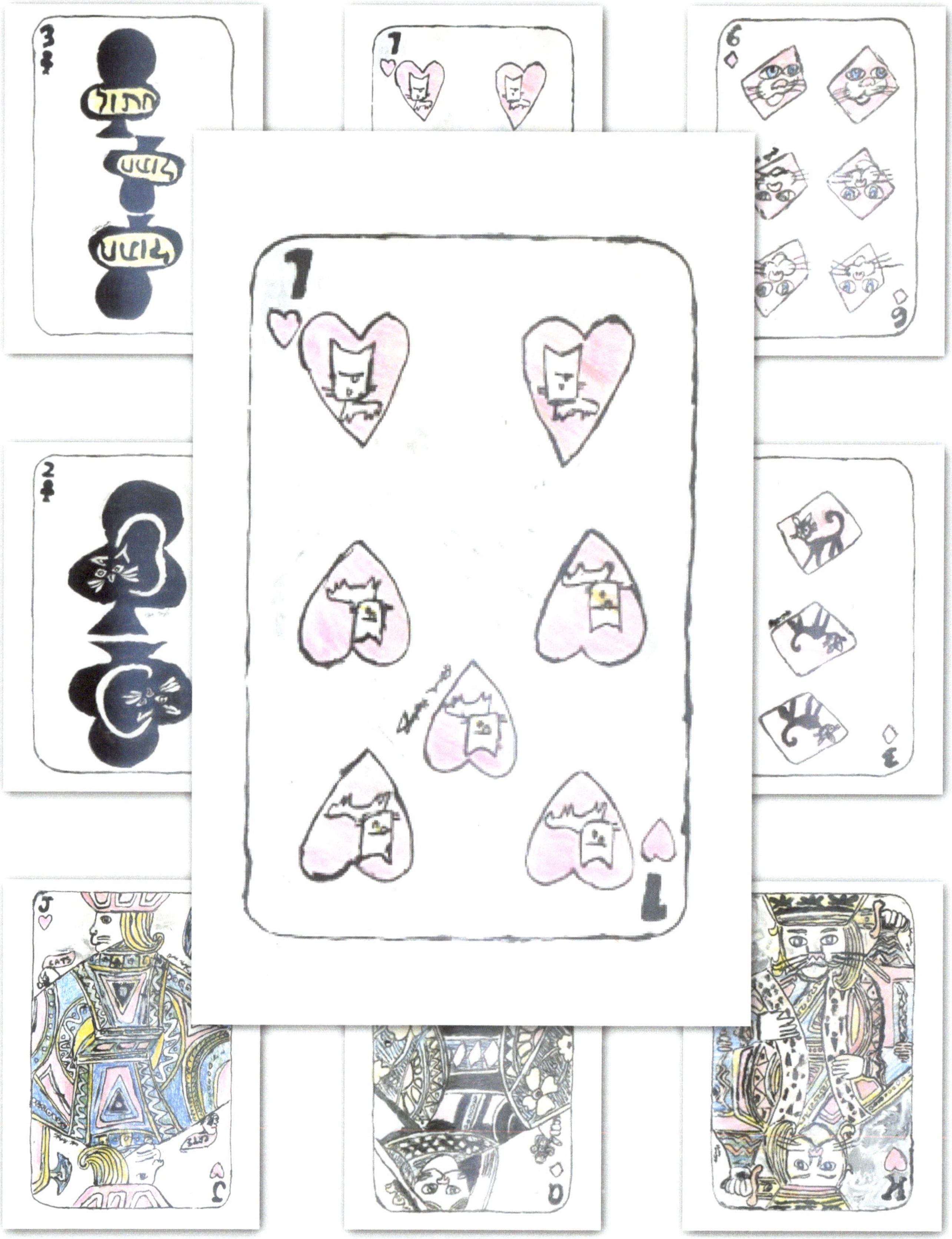

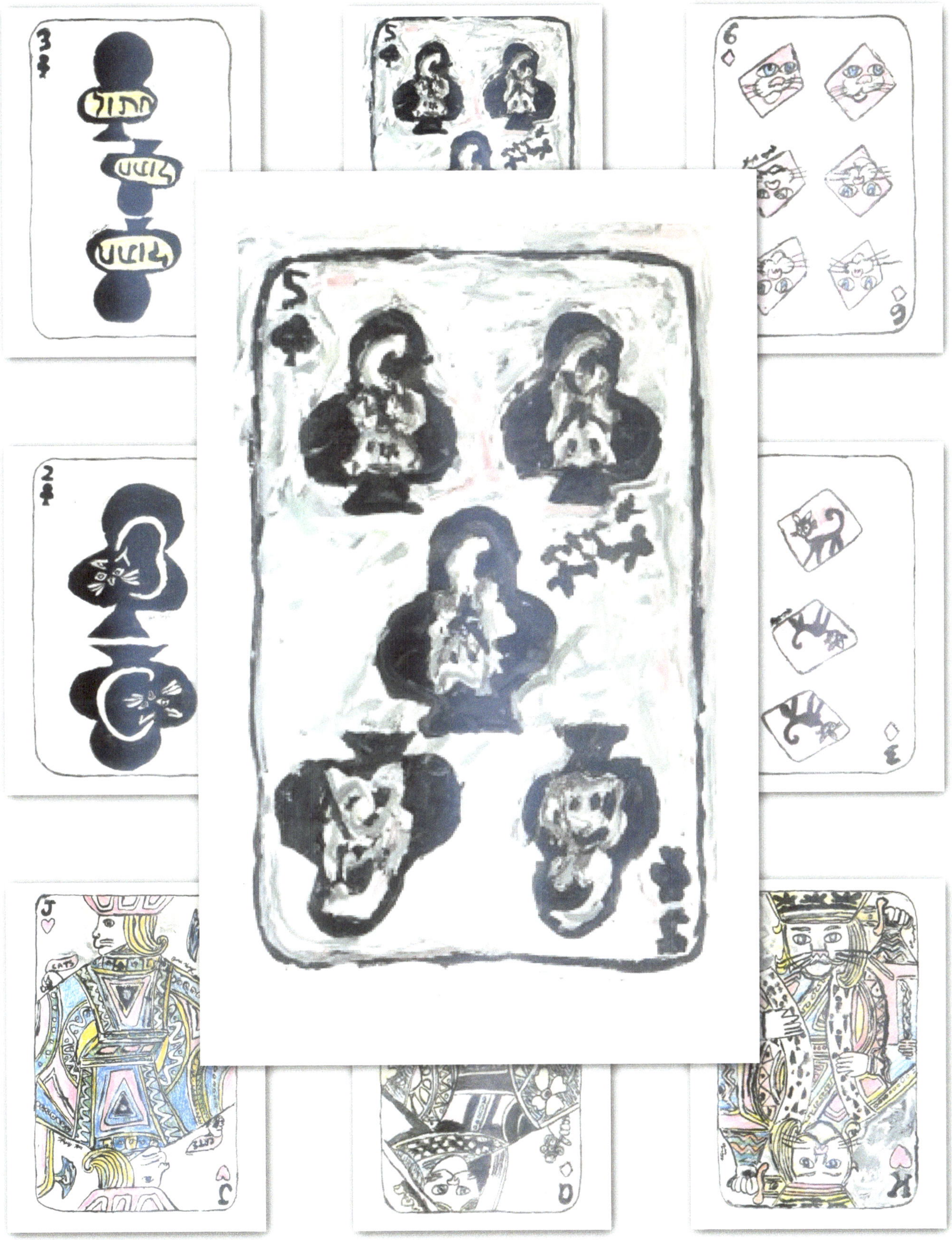

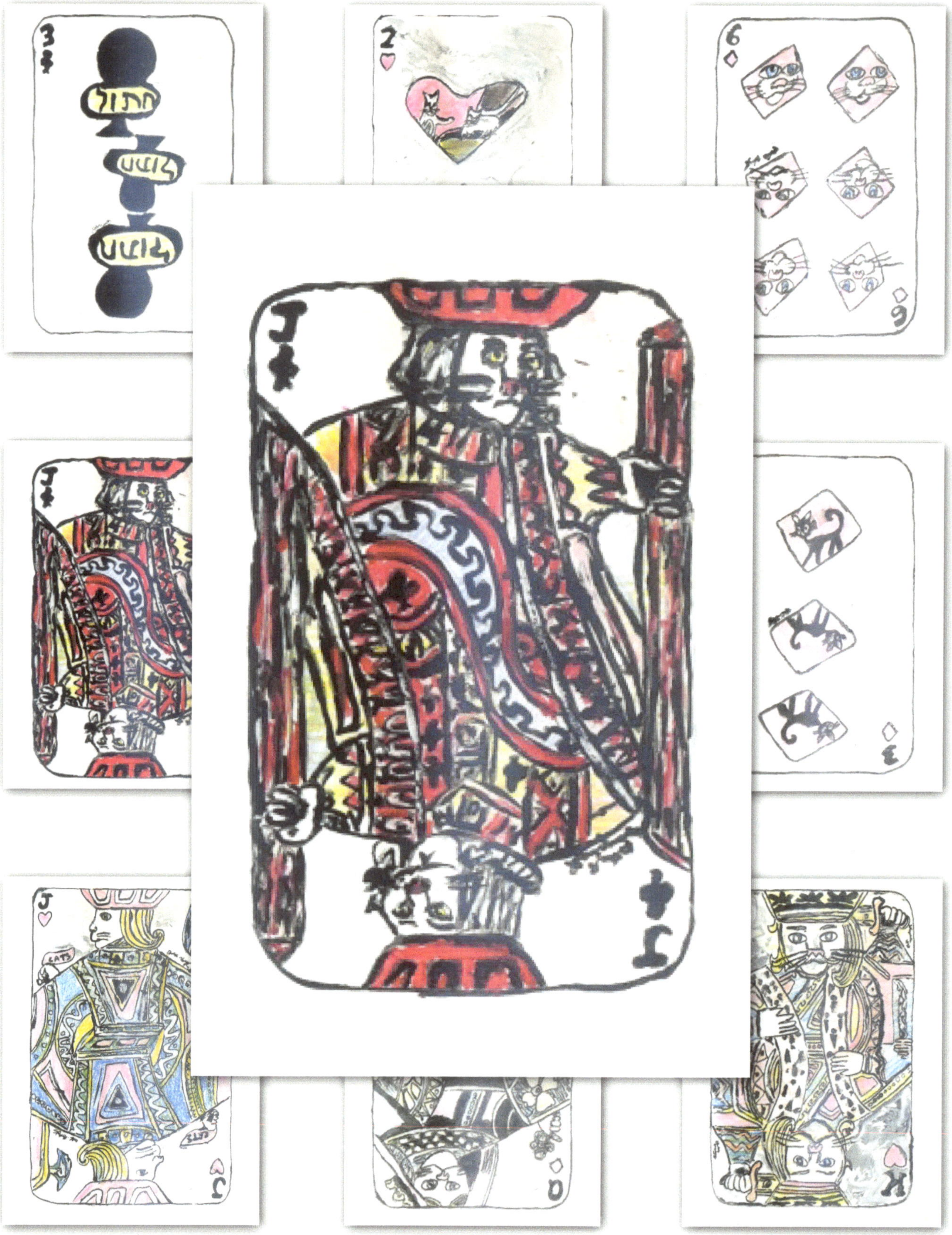

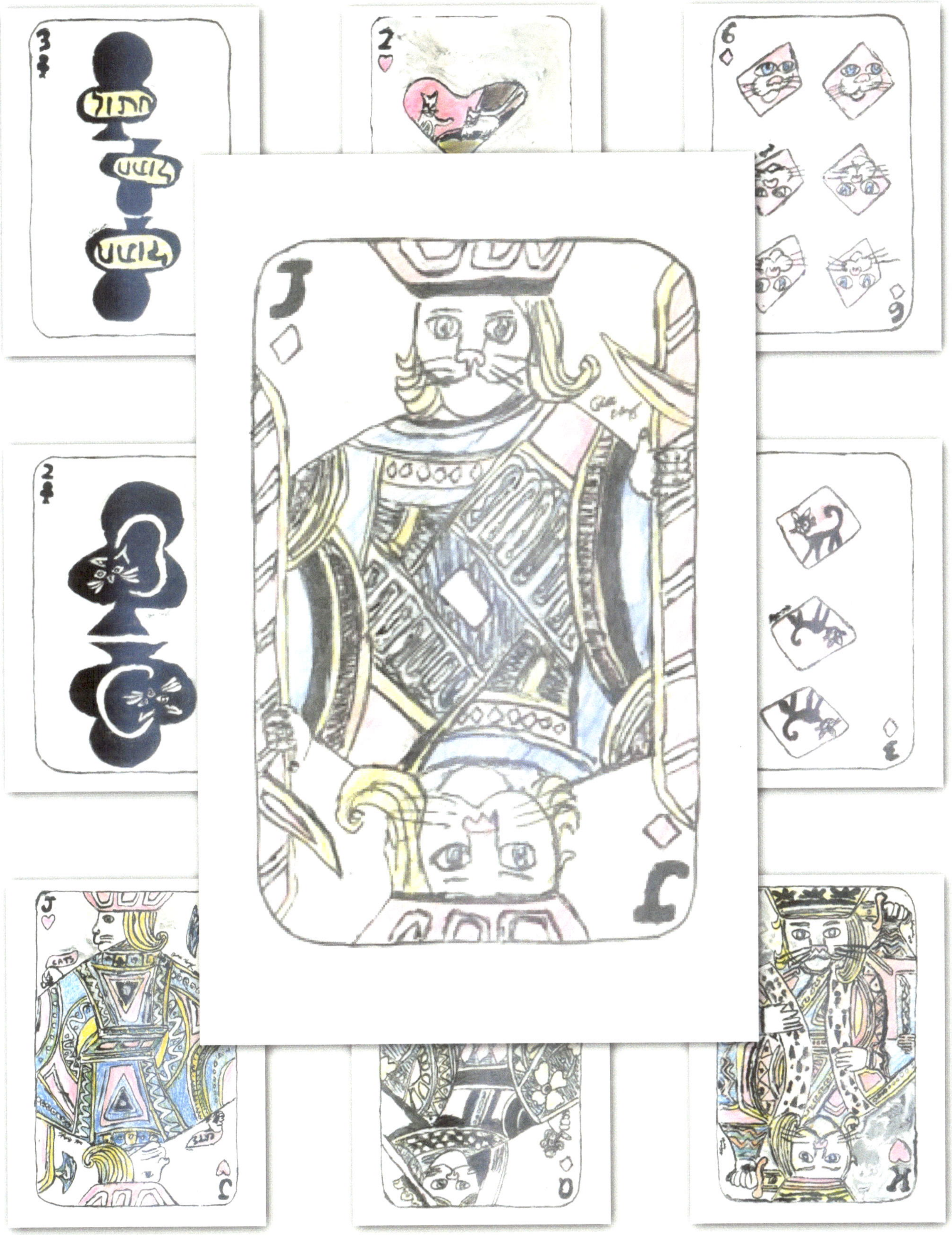

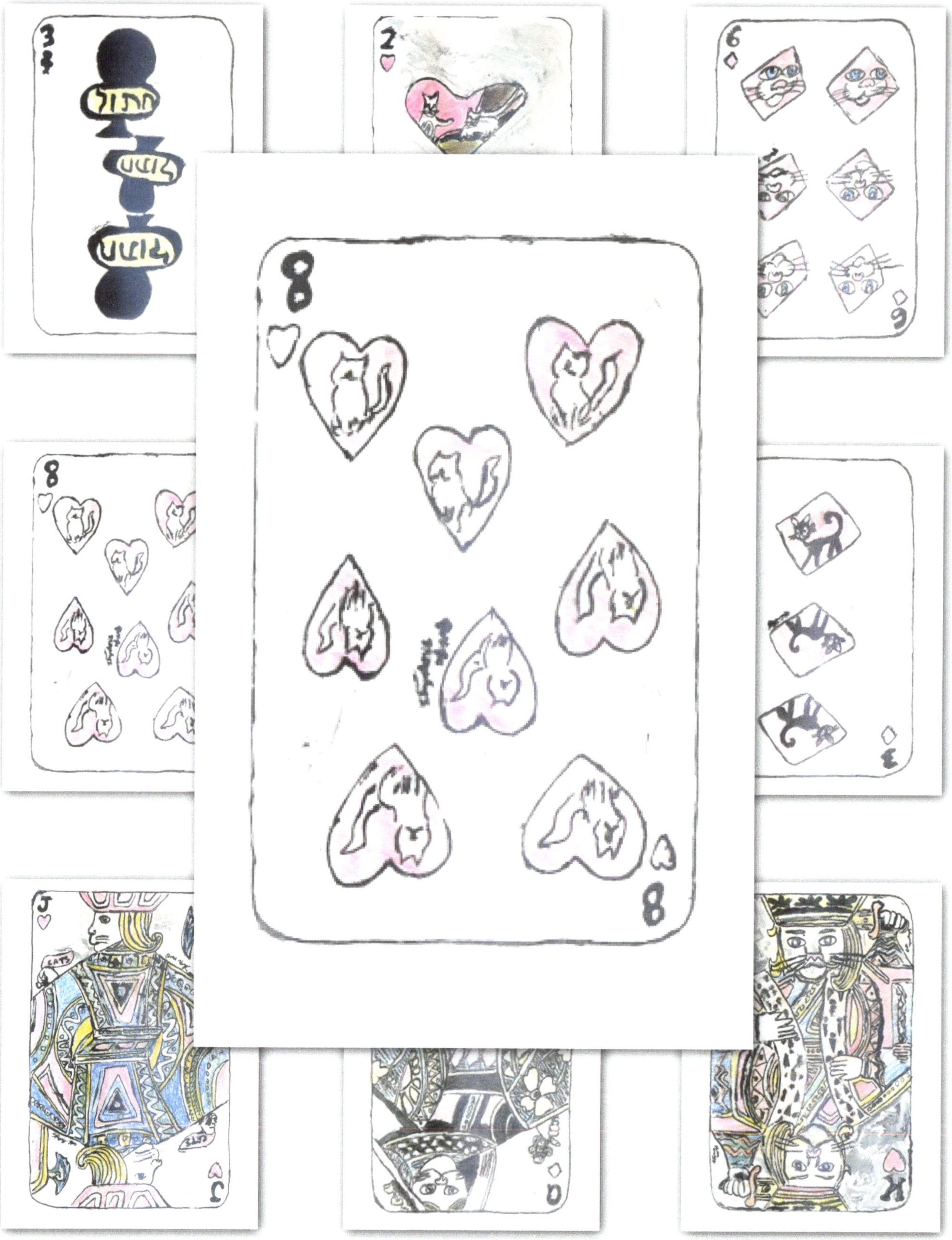

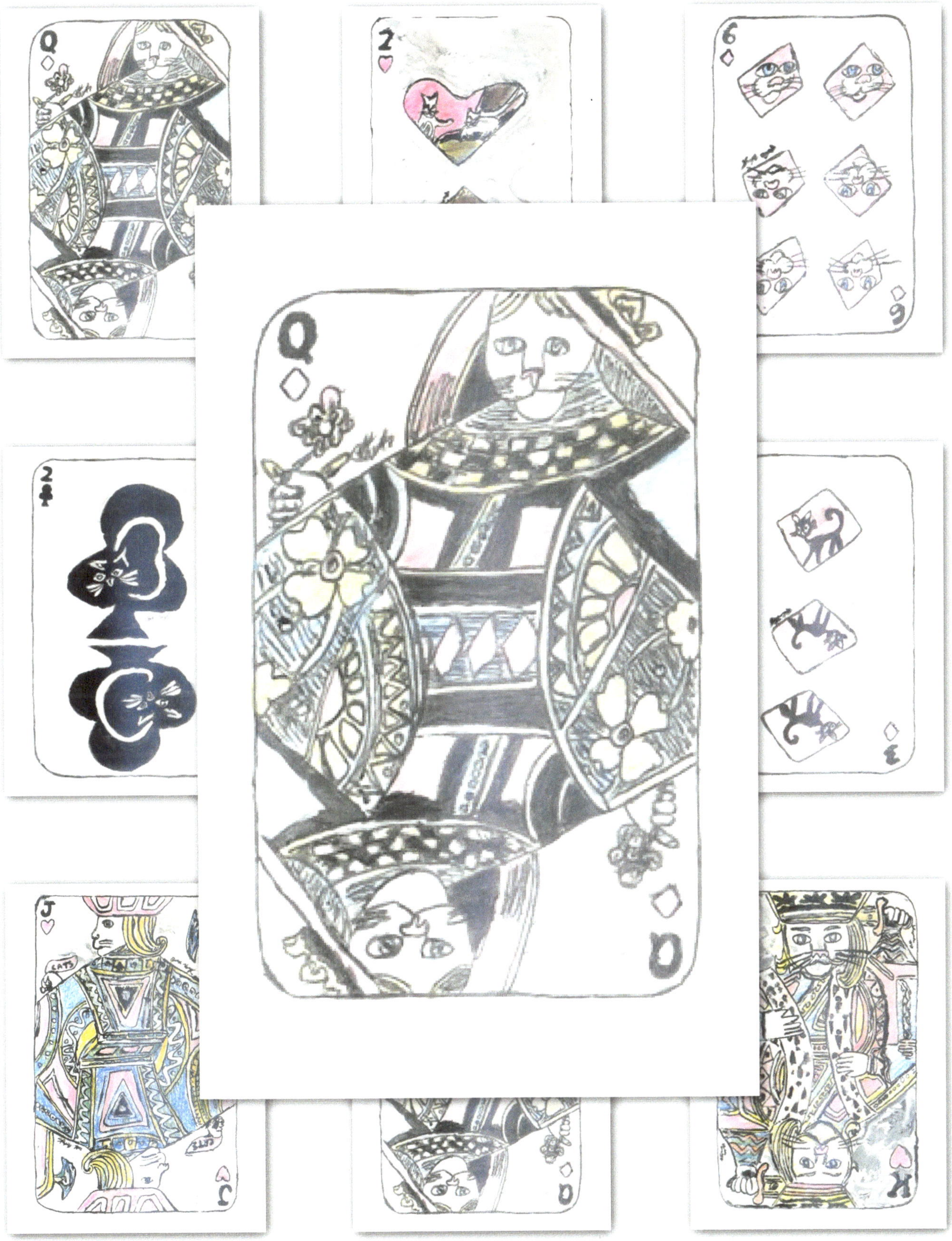

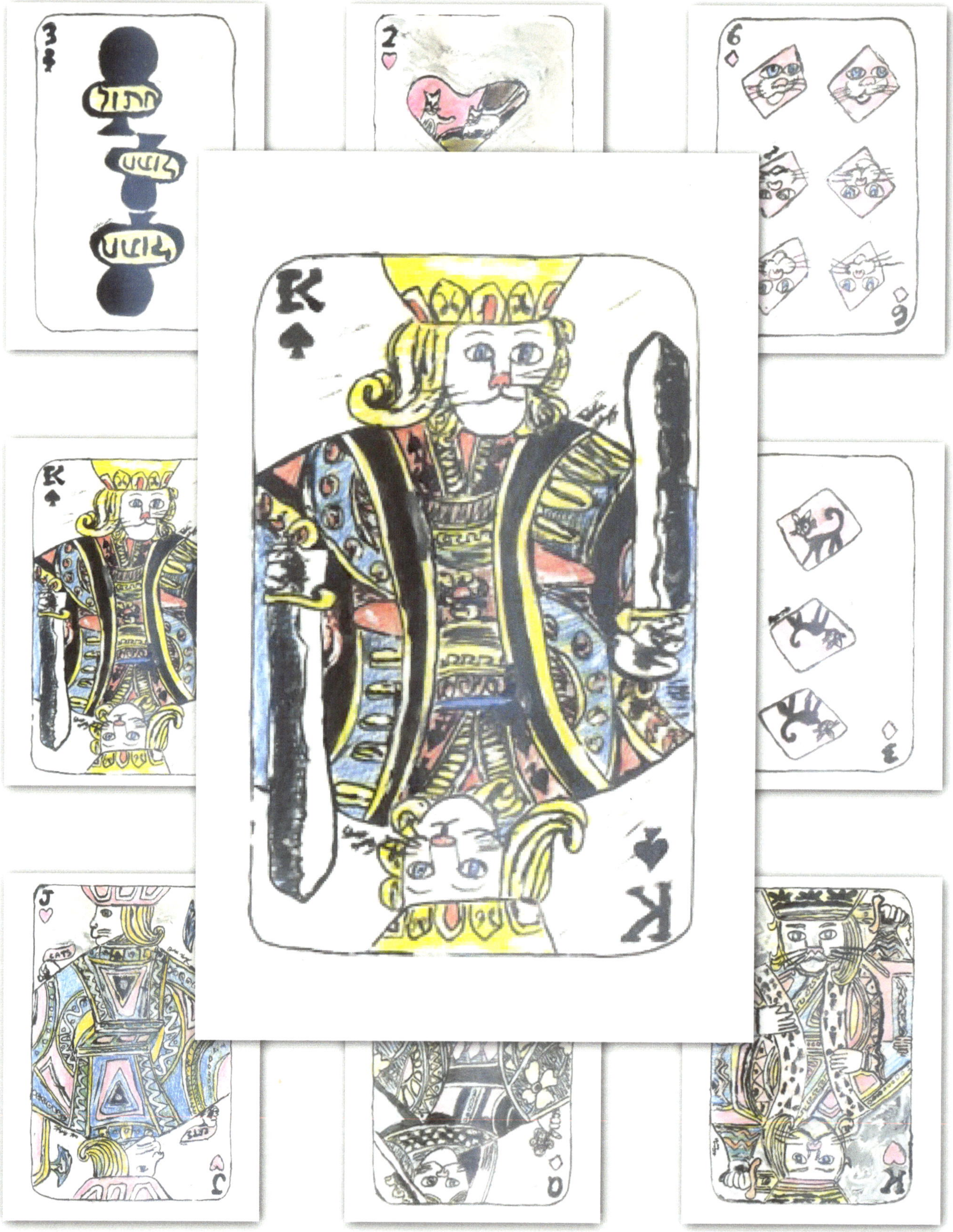

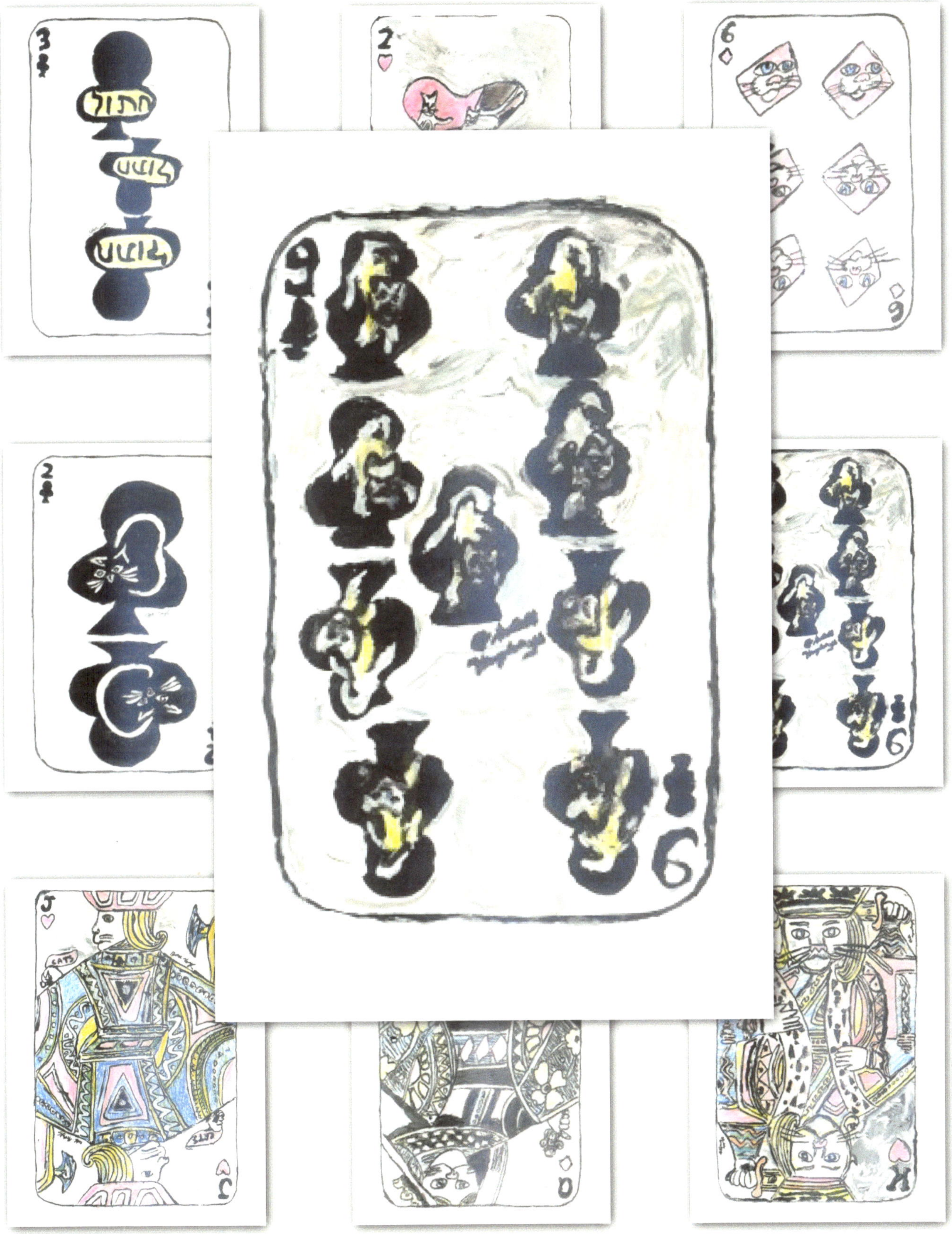

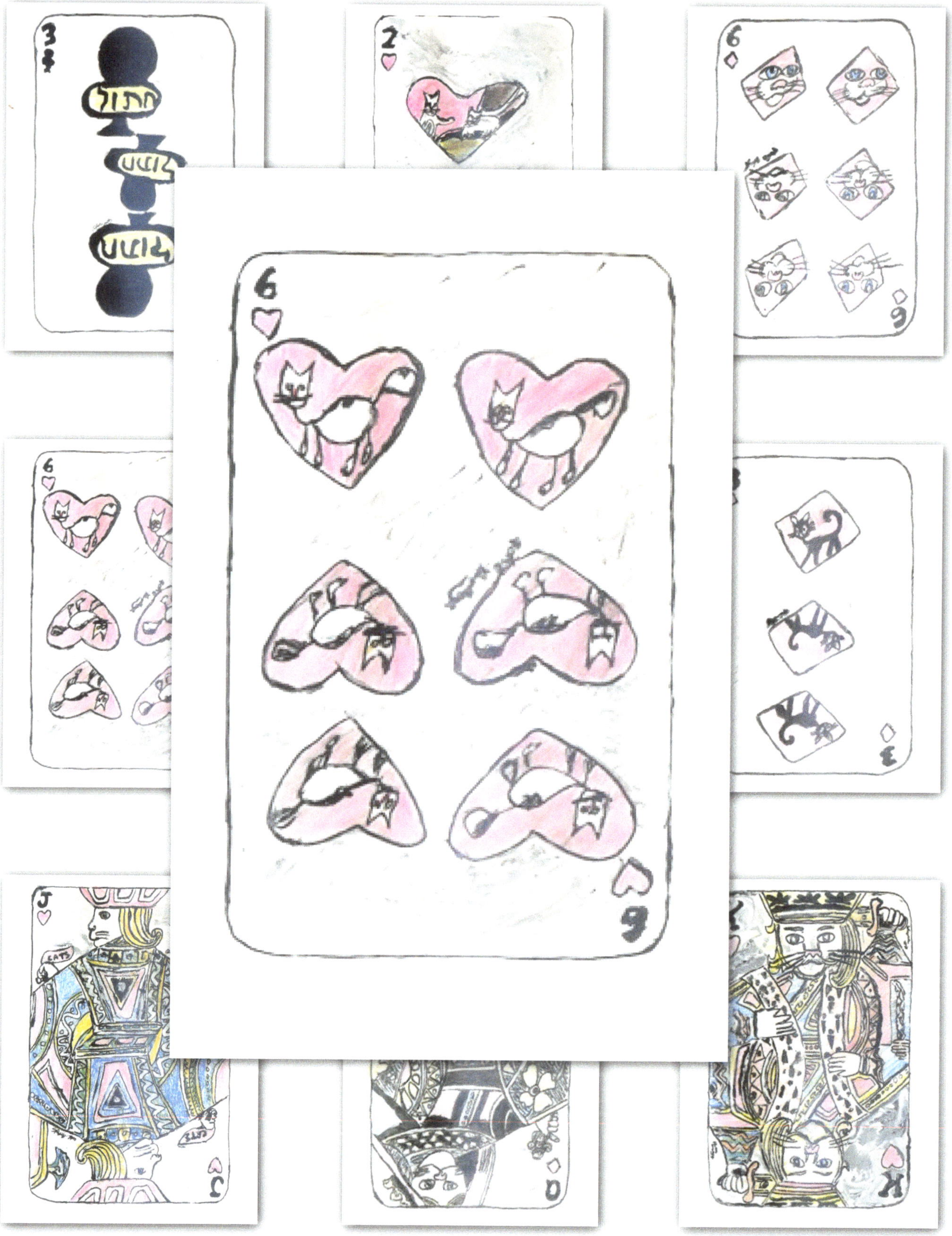

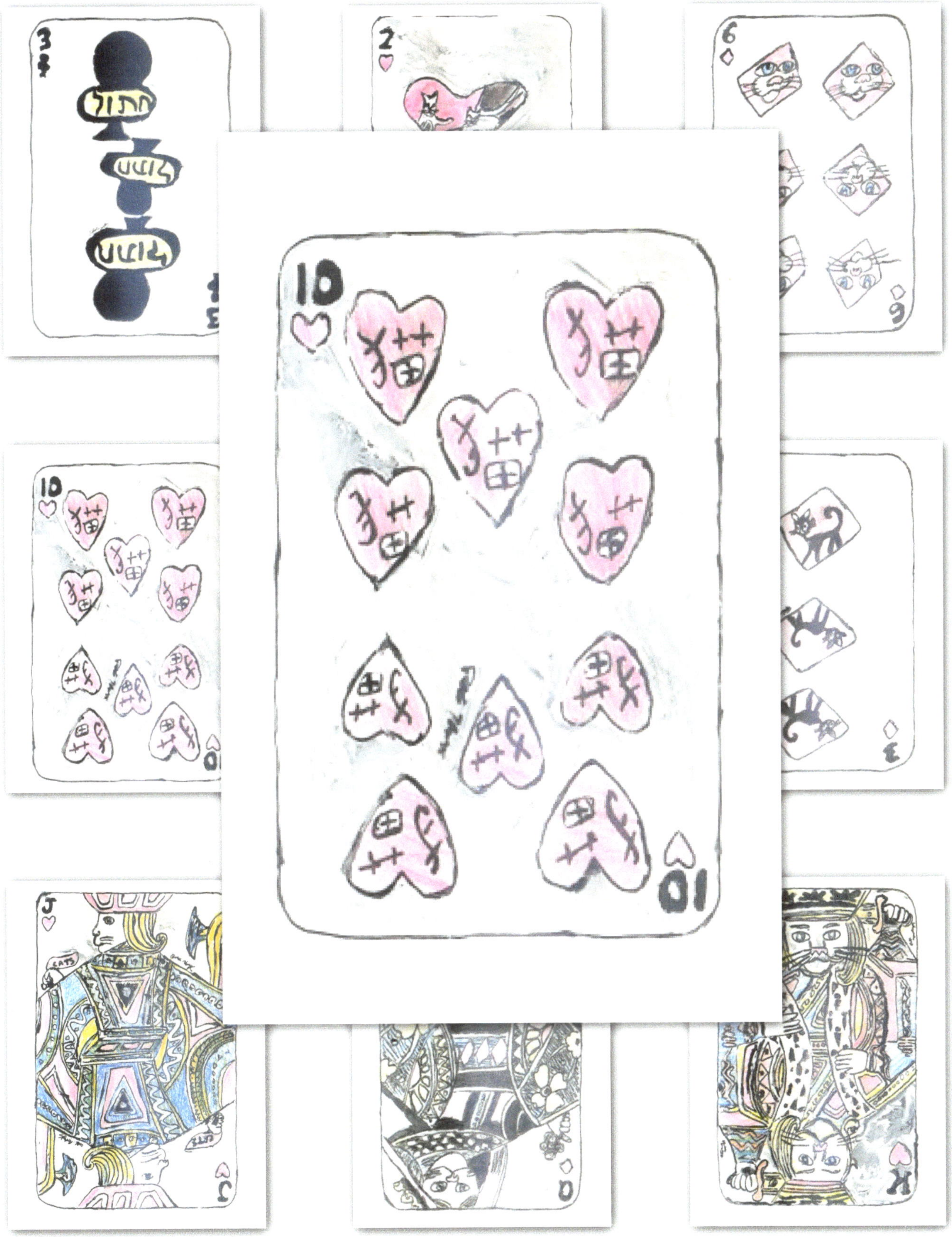

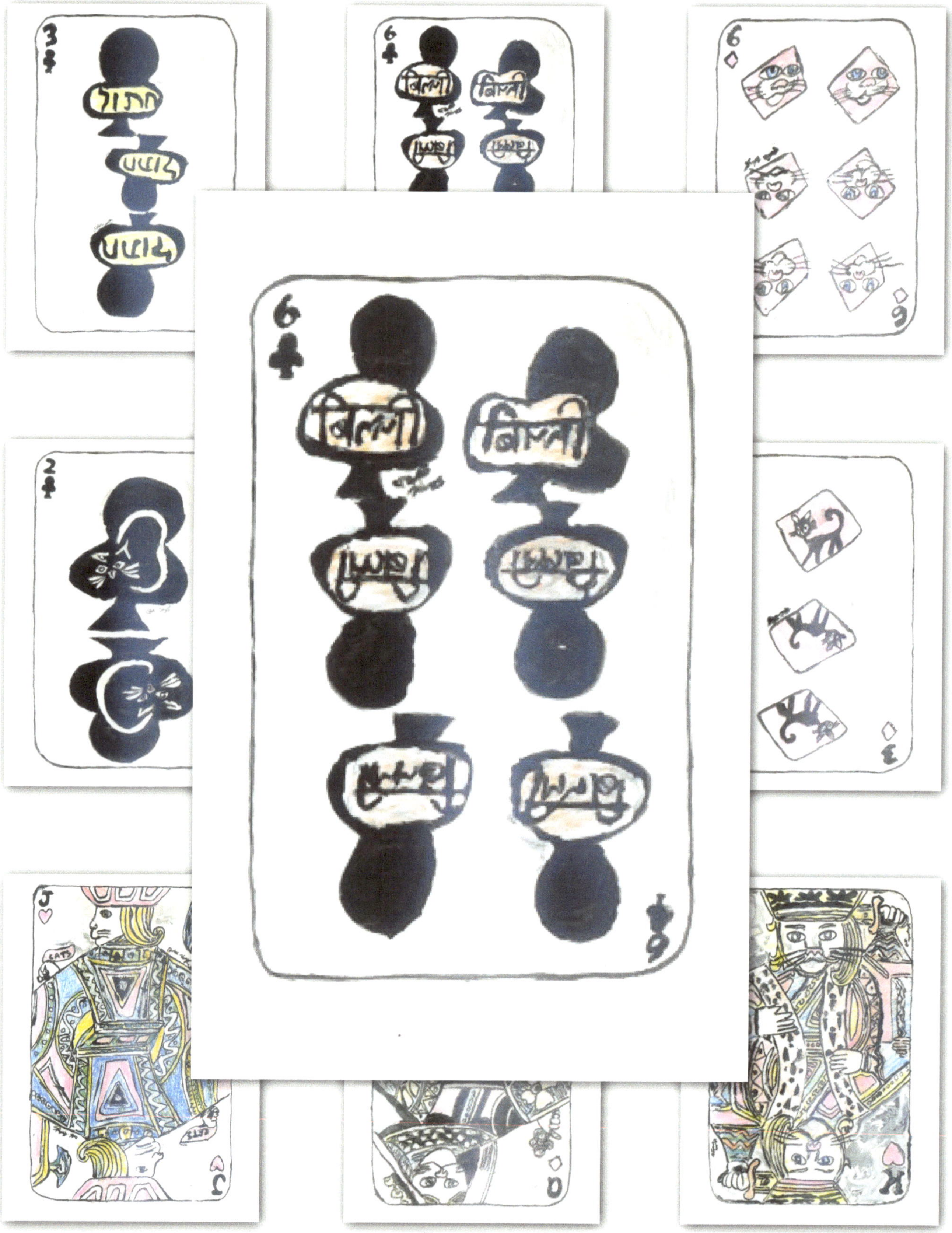

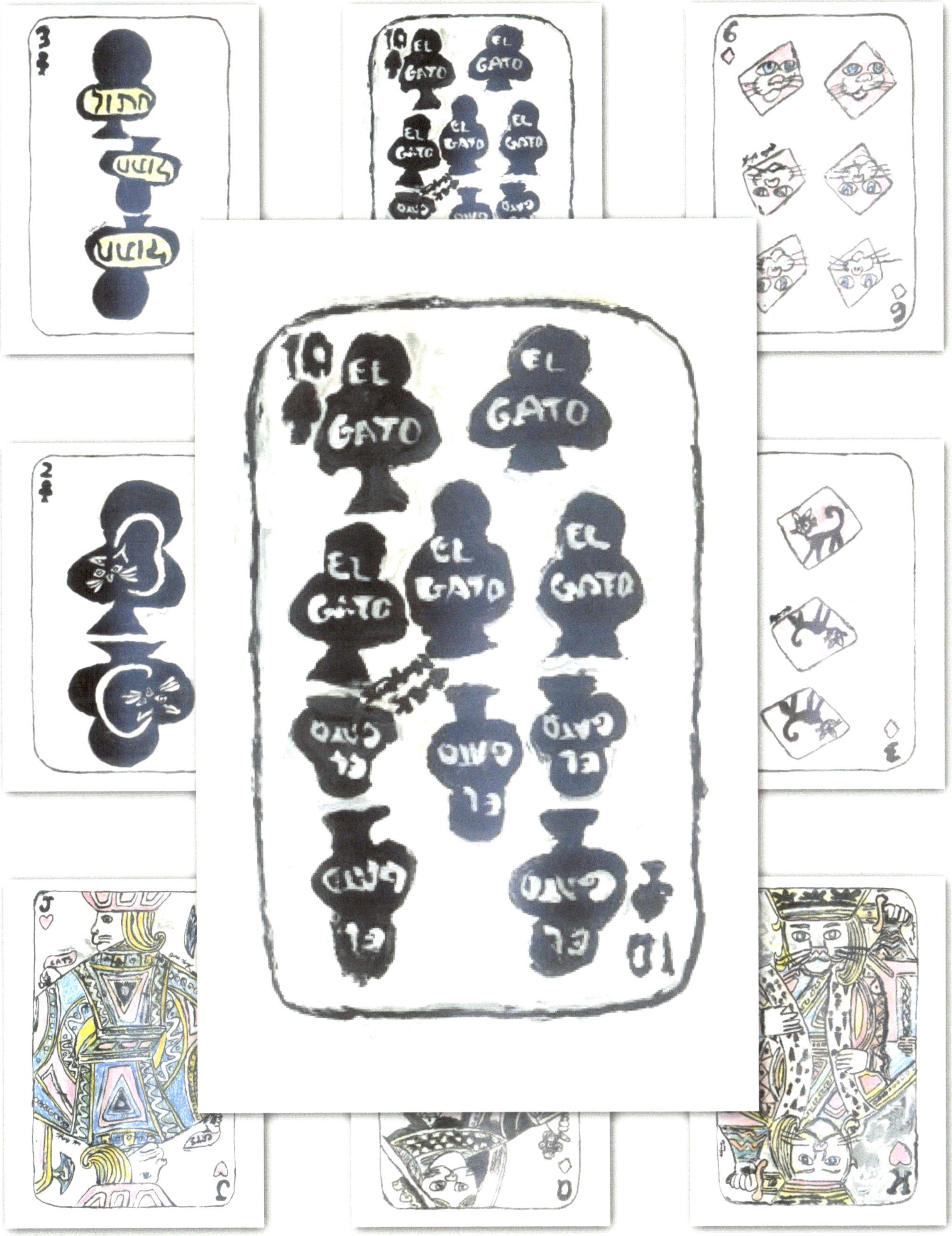
10
EL
GATO

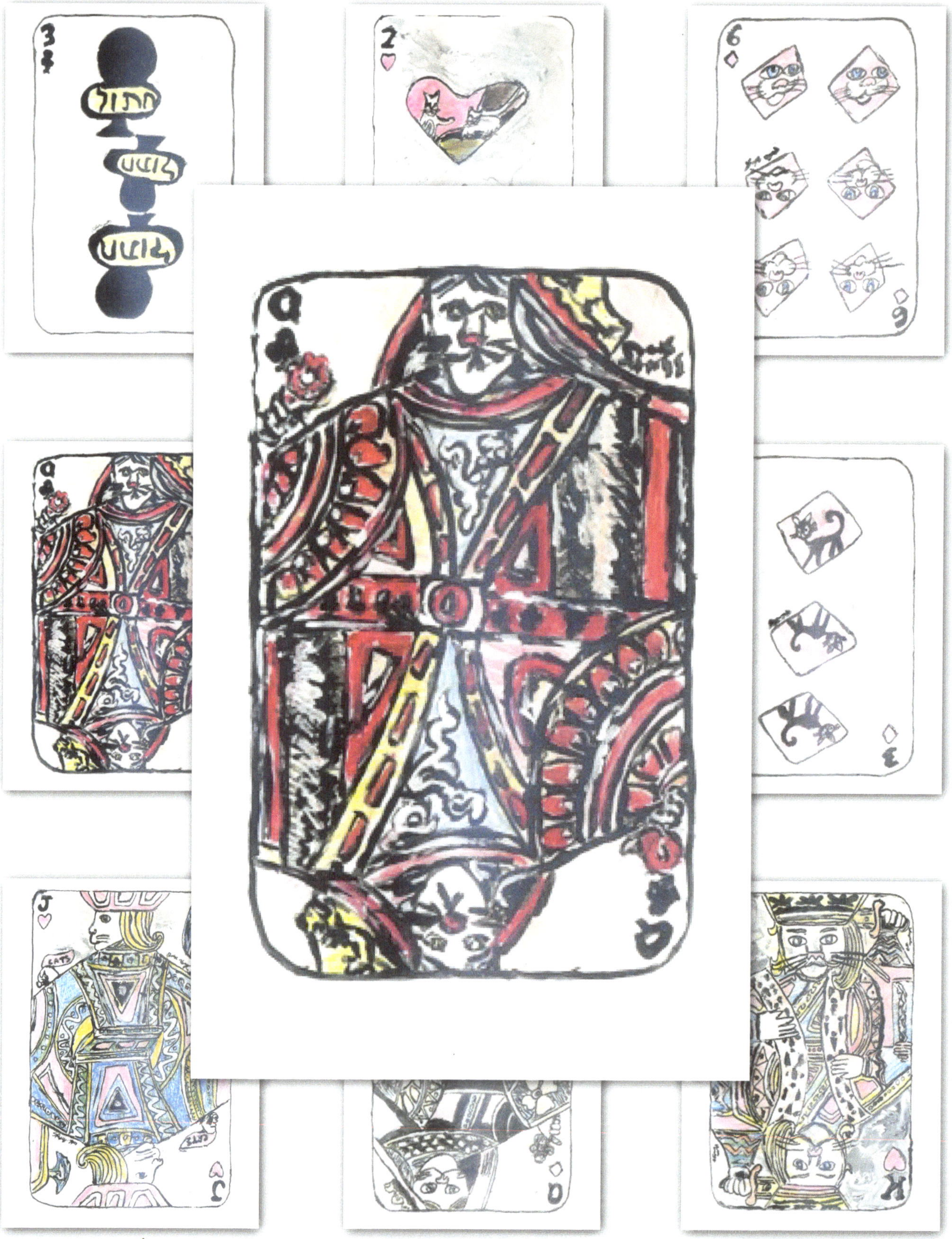

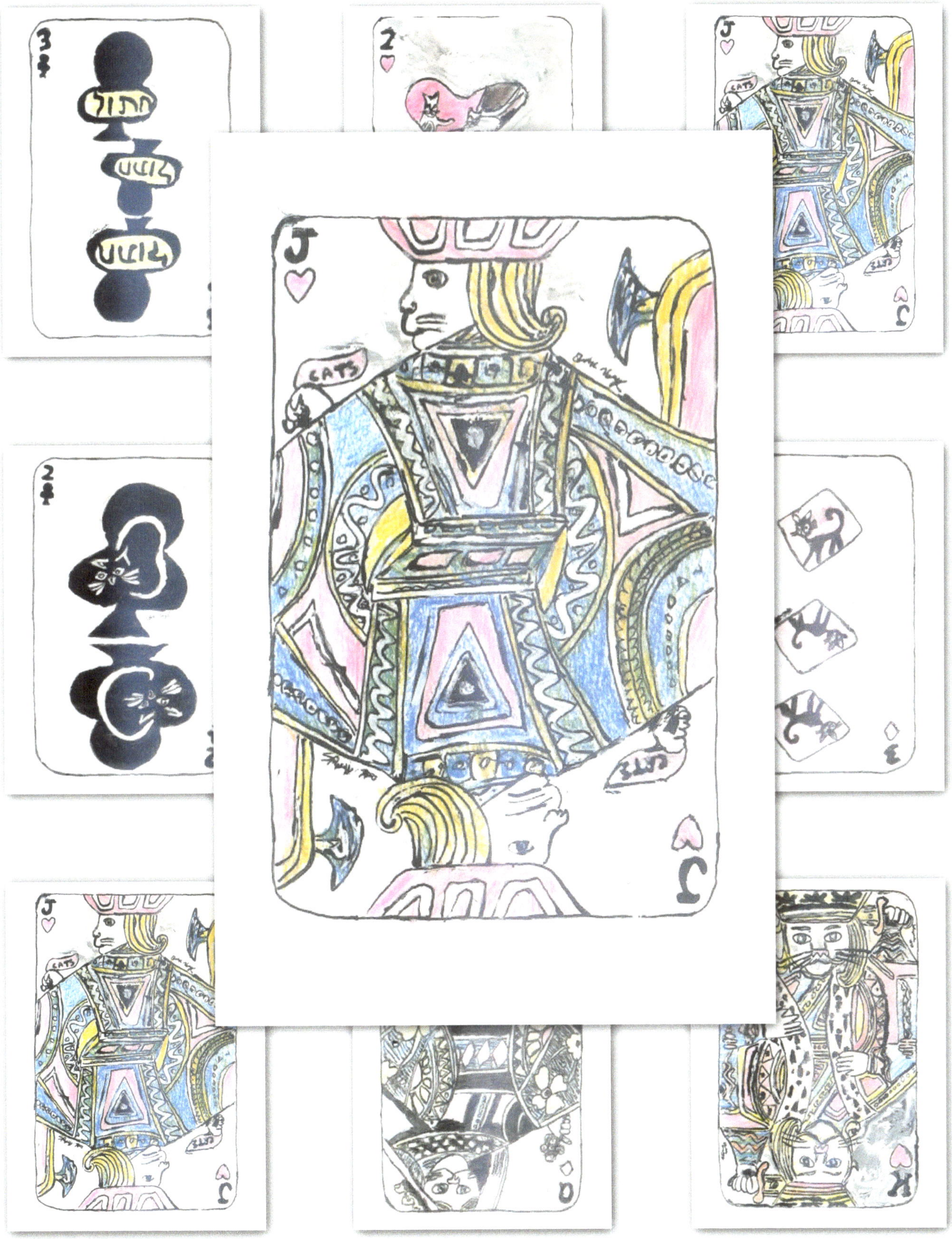
CATS

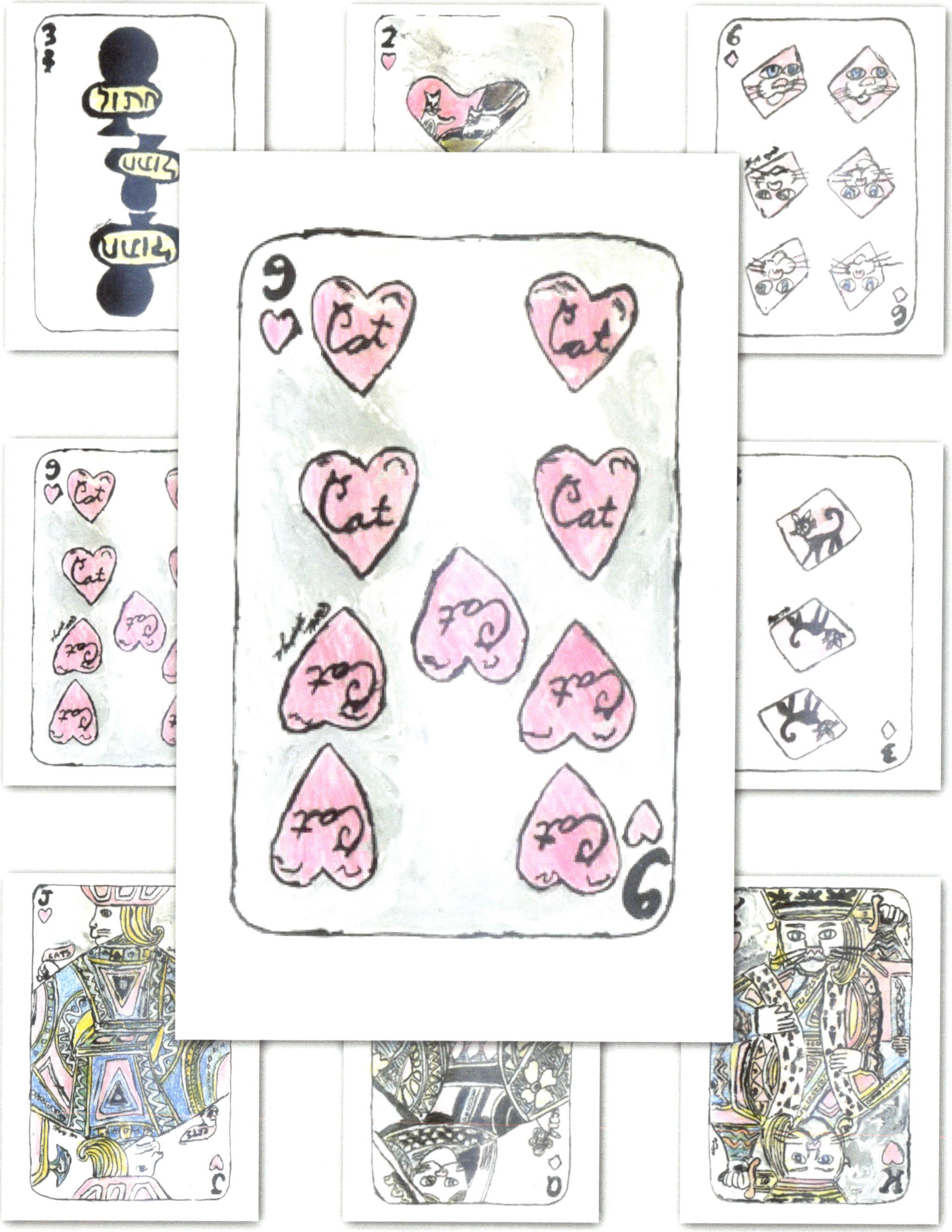
Cat
Cat
Cat
Cat

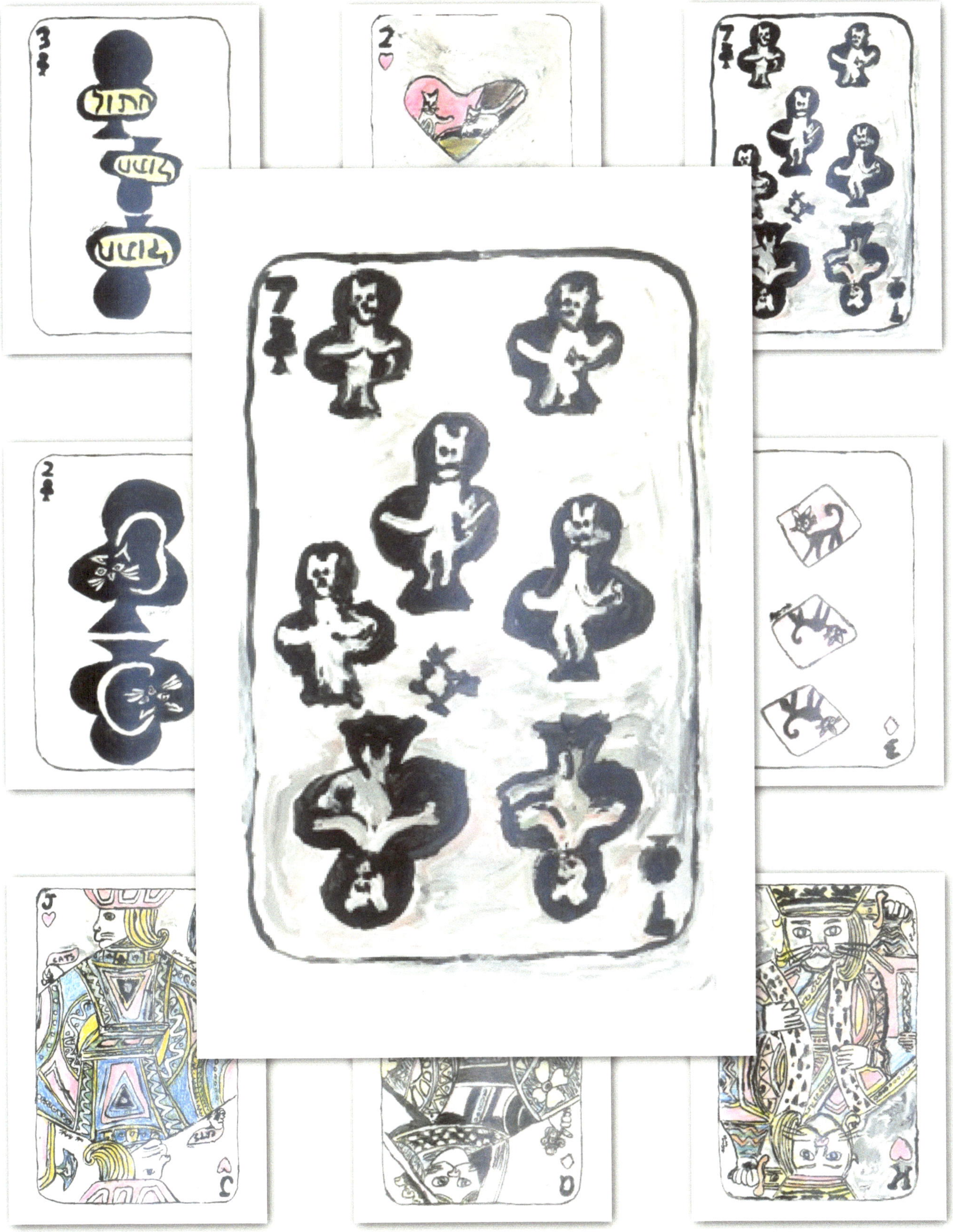
חתול

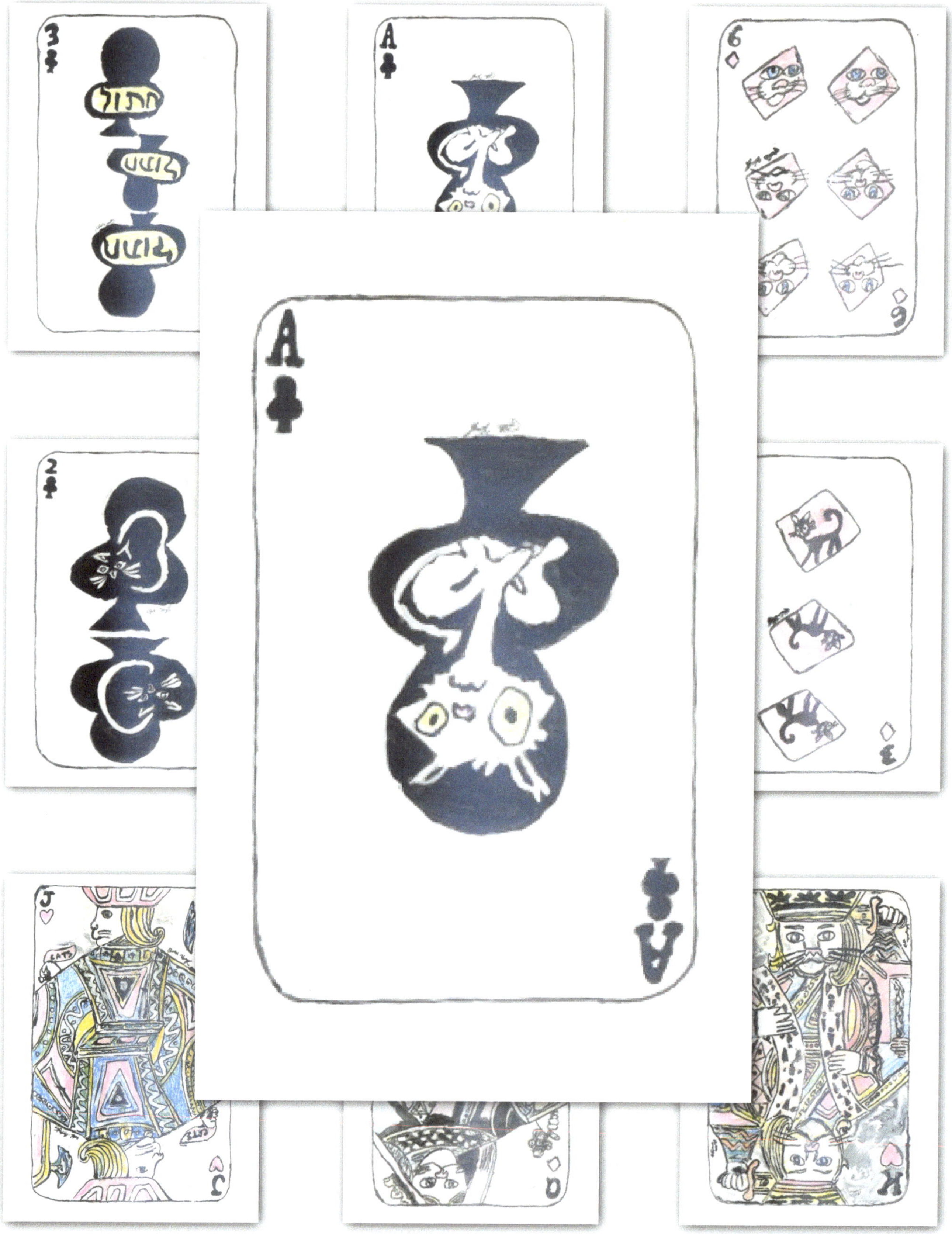

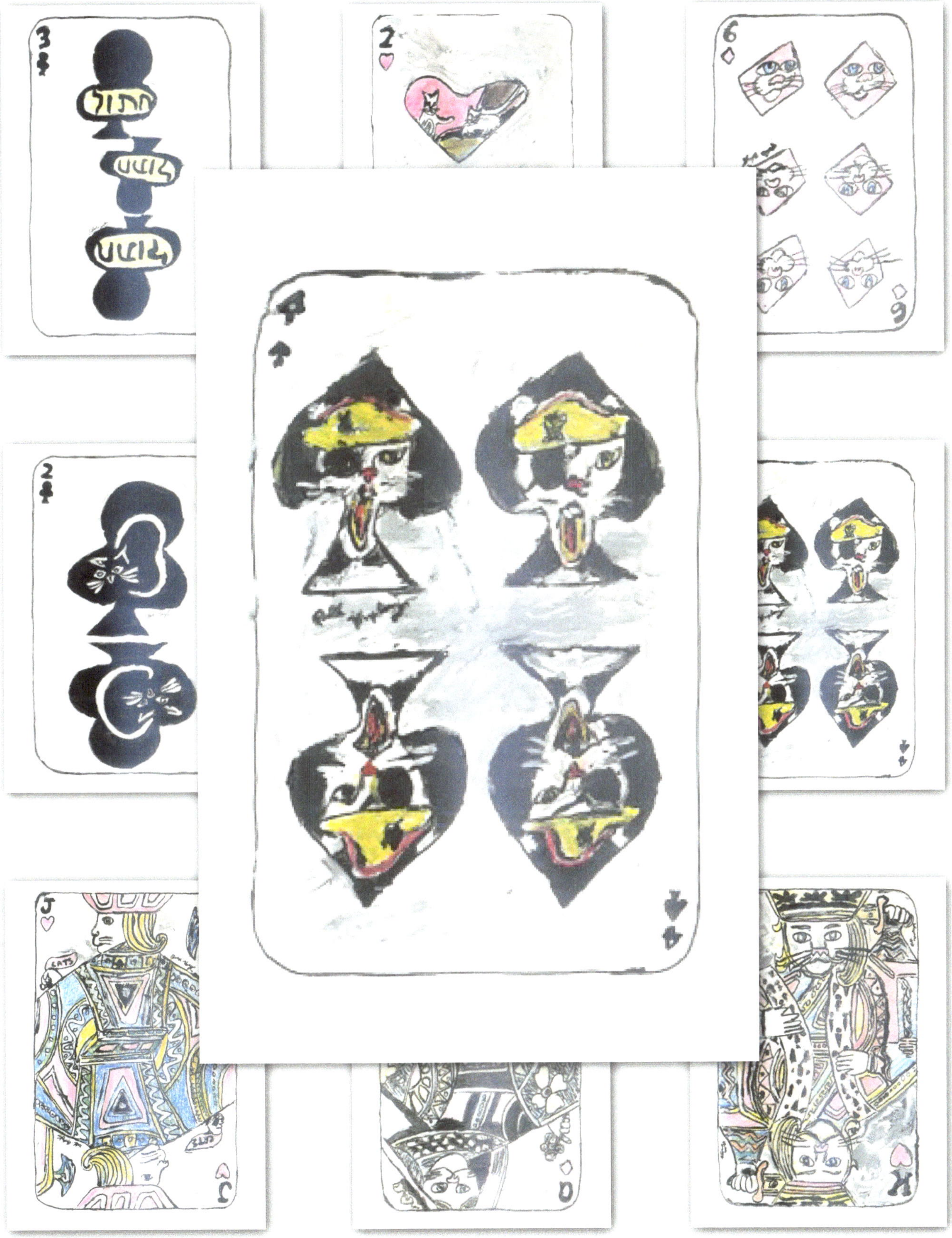

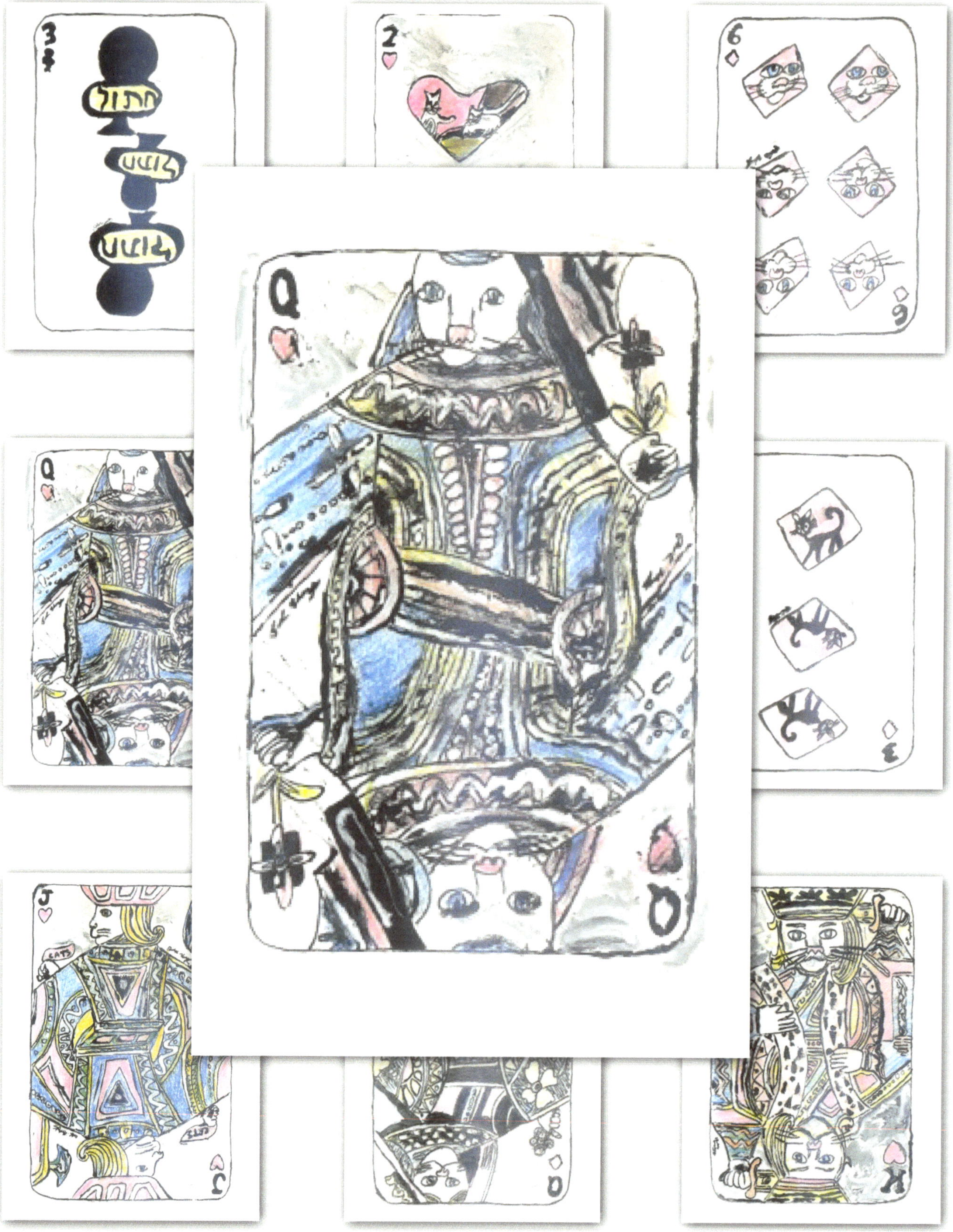

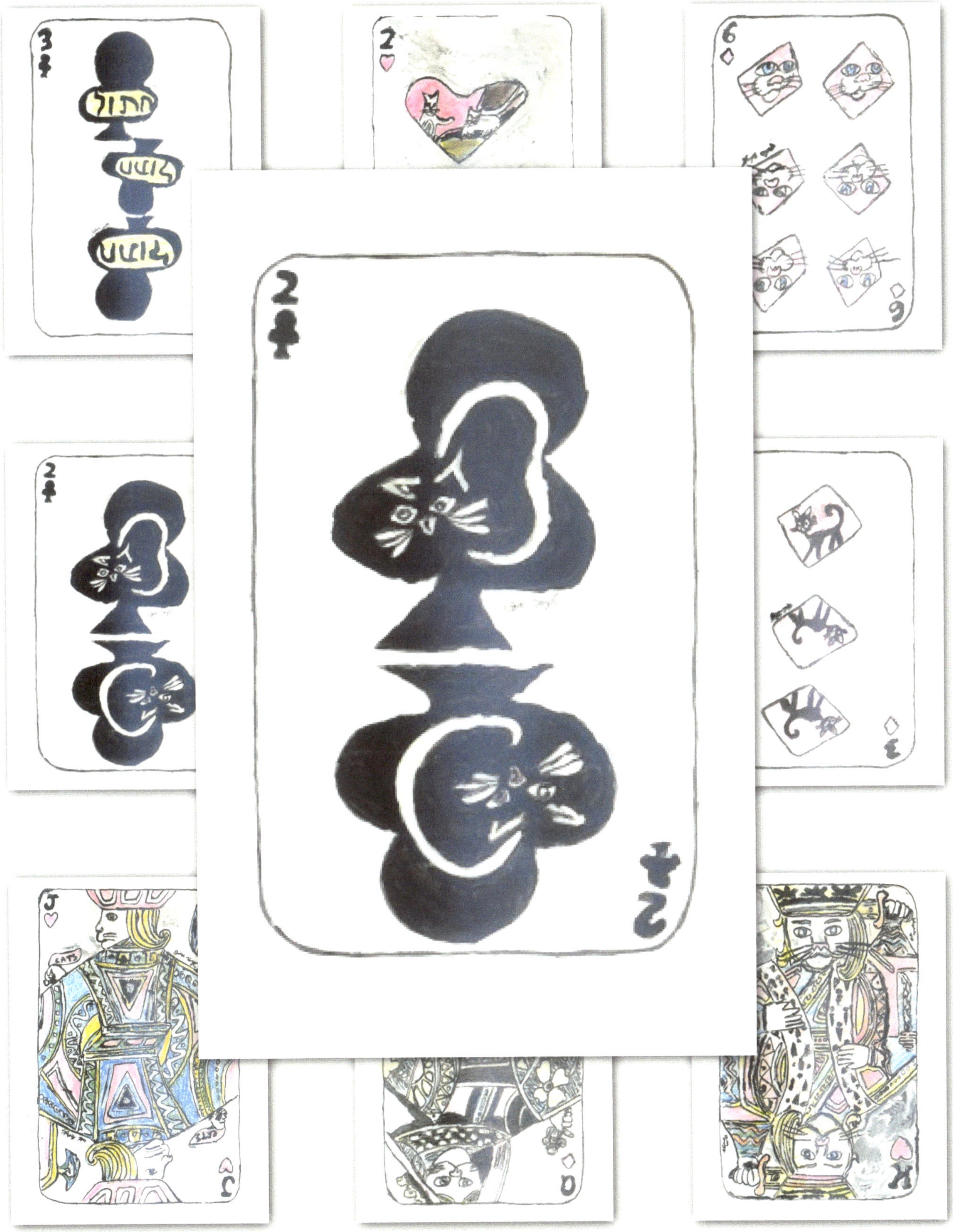

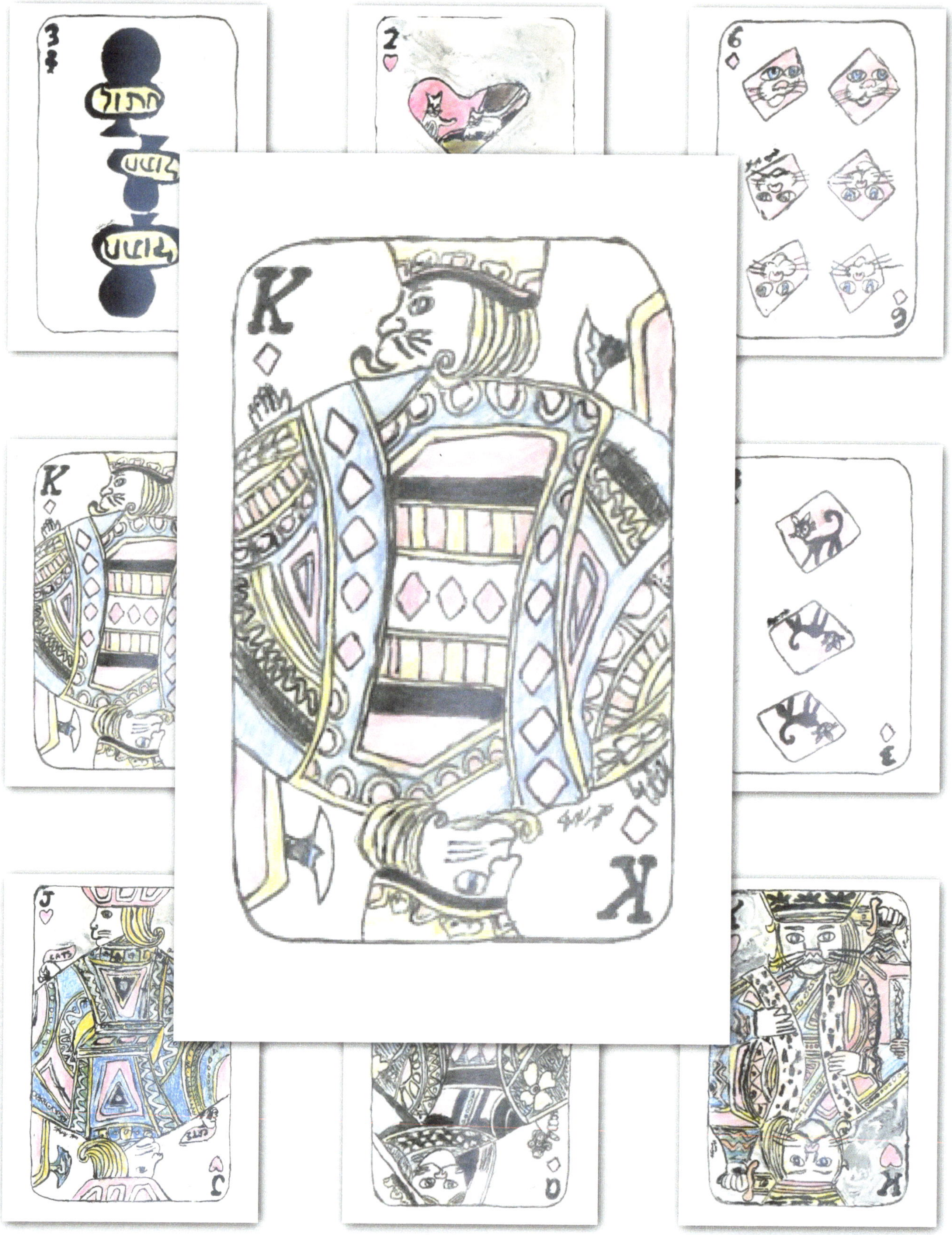

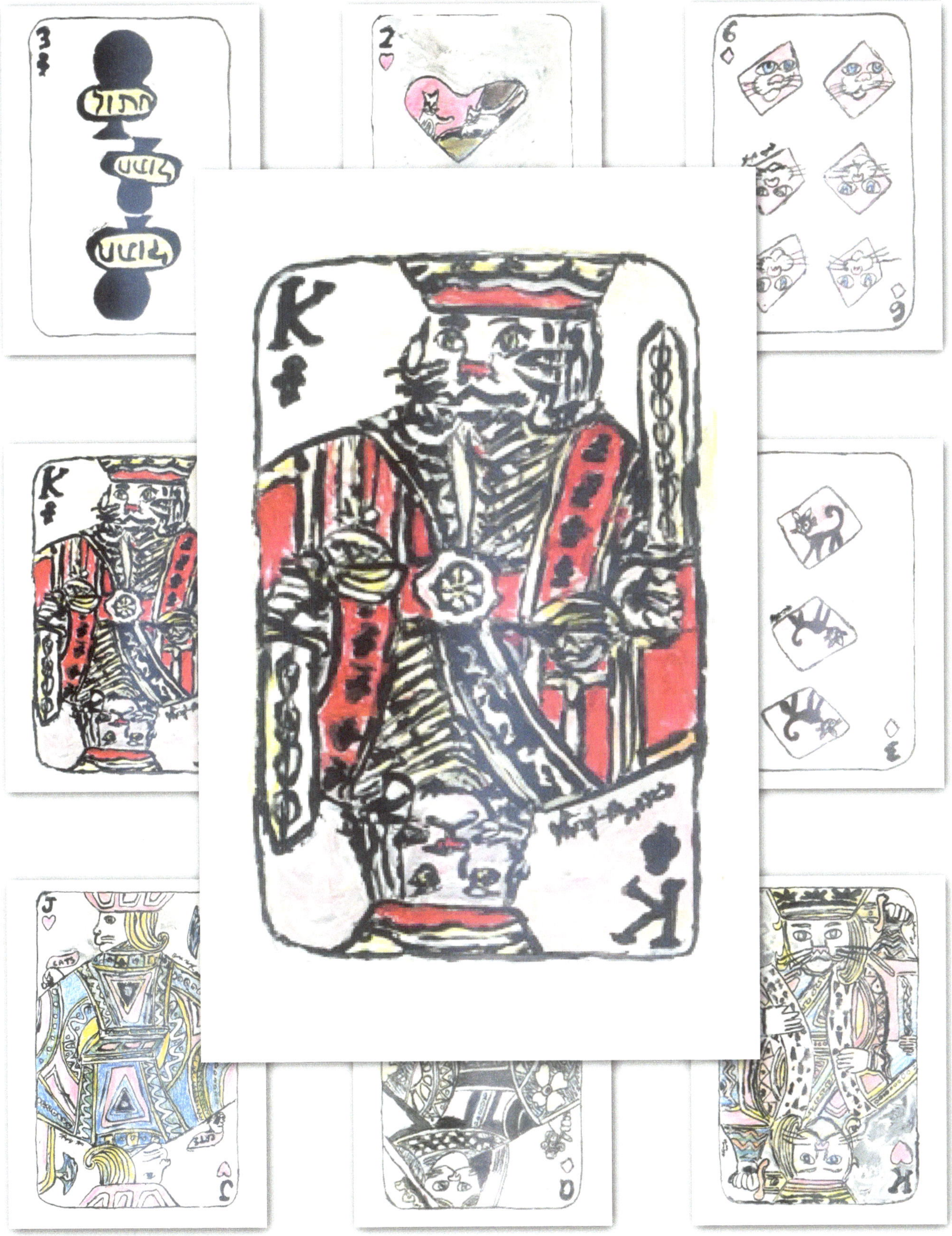

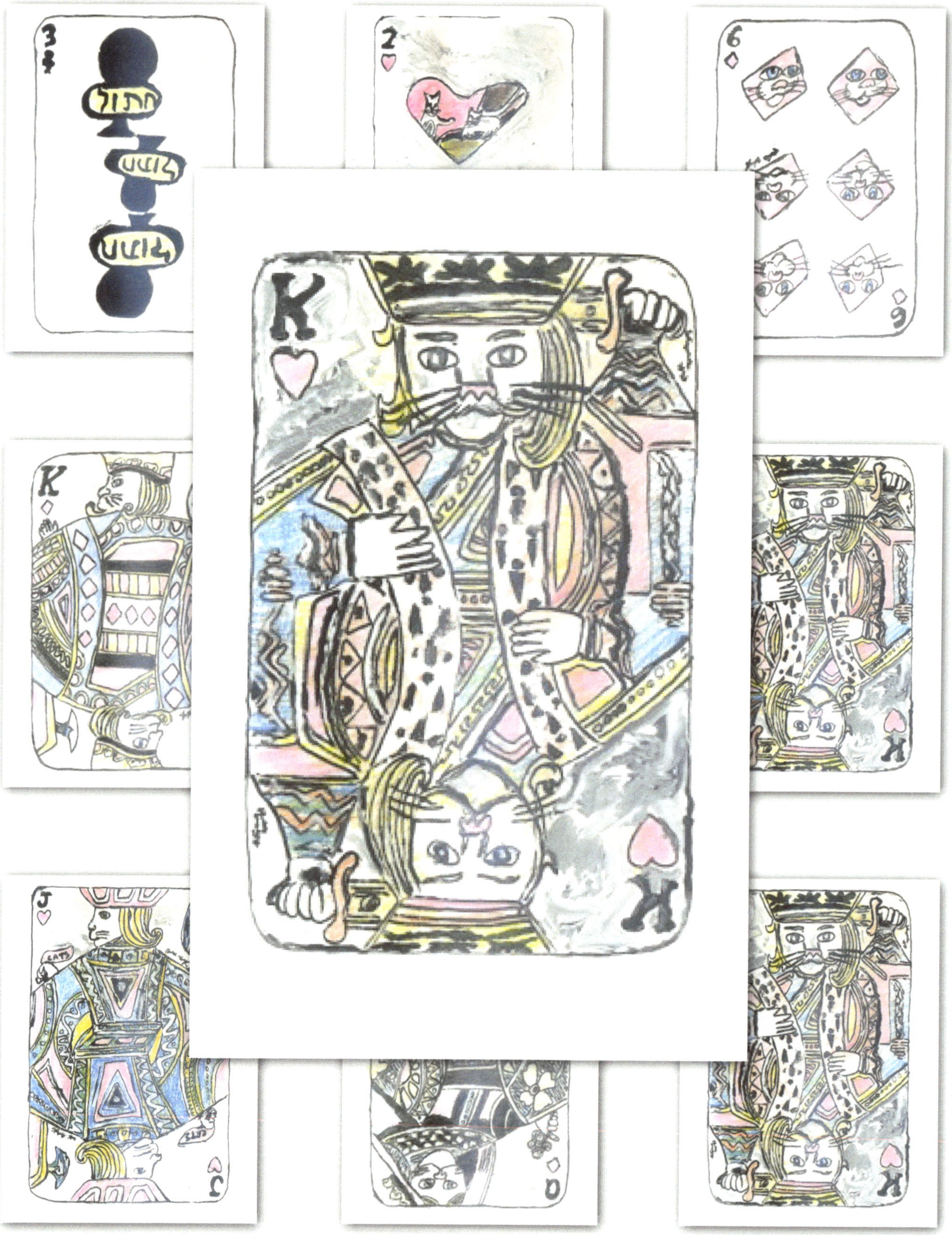

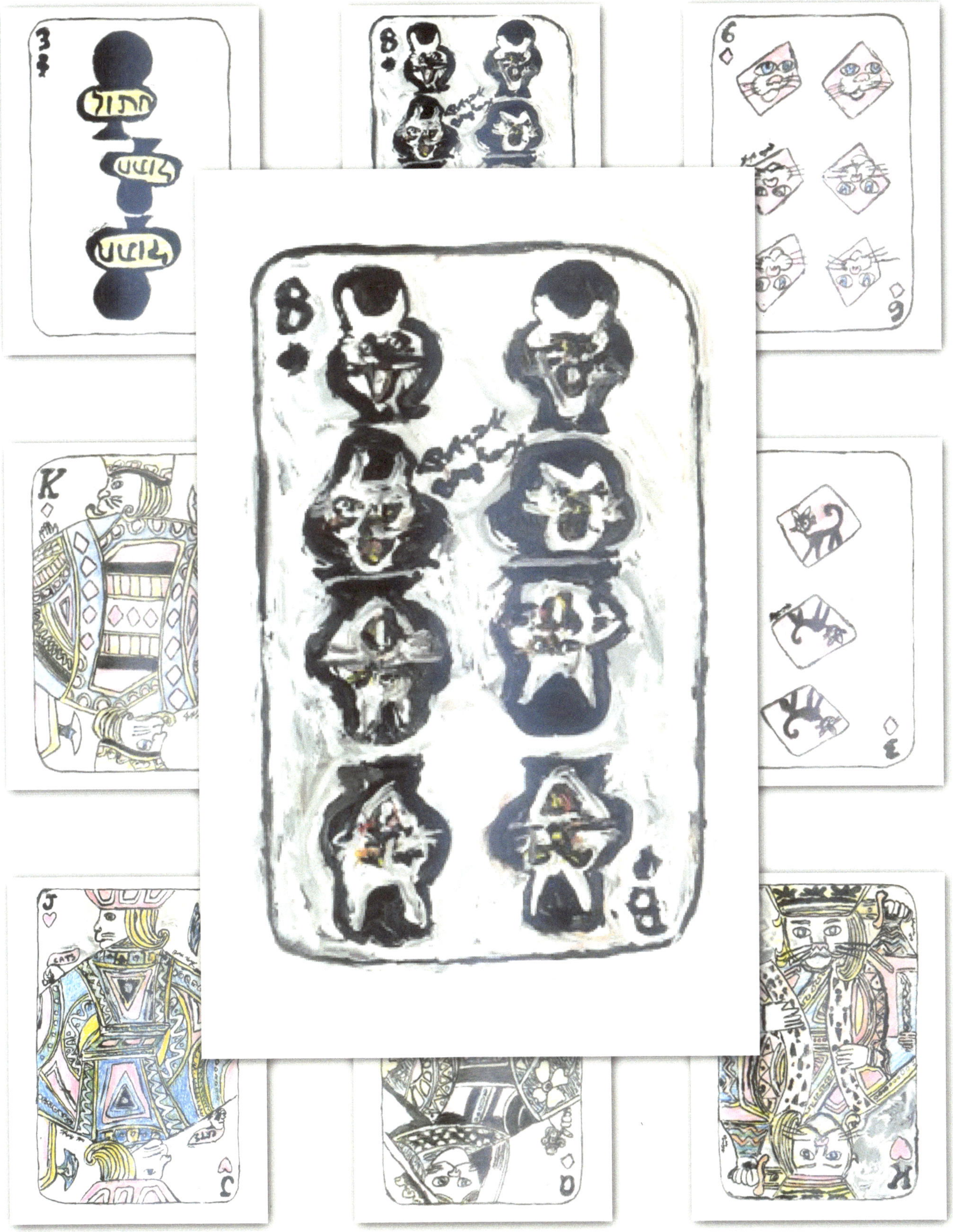

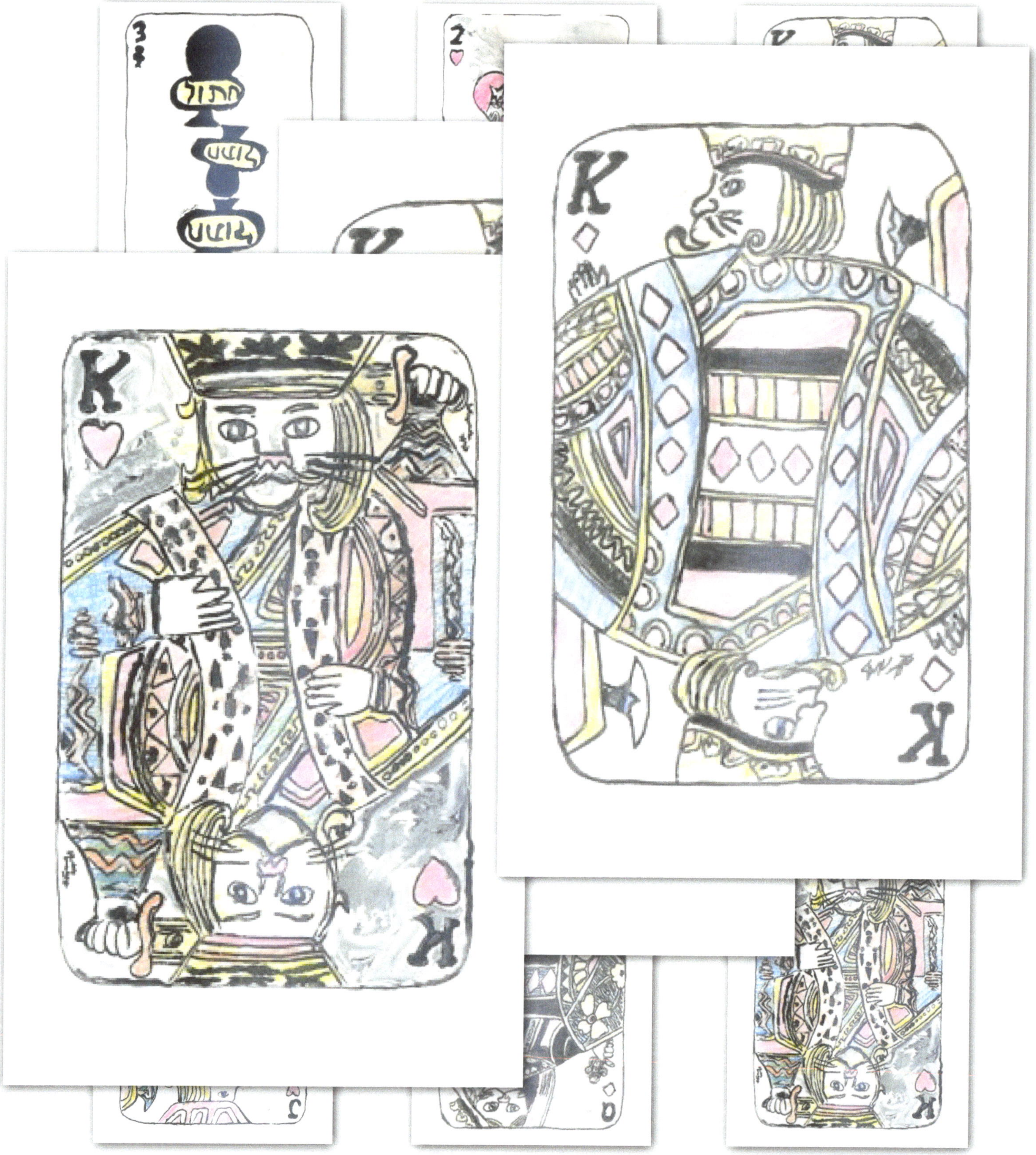

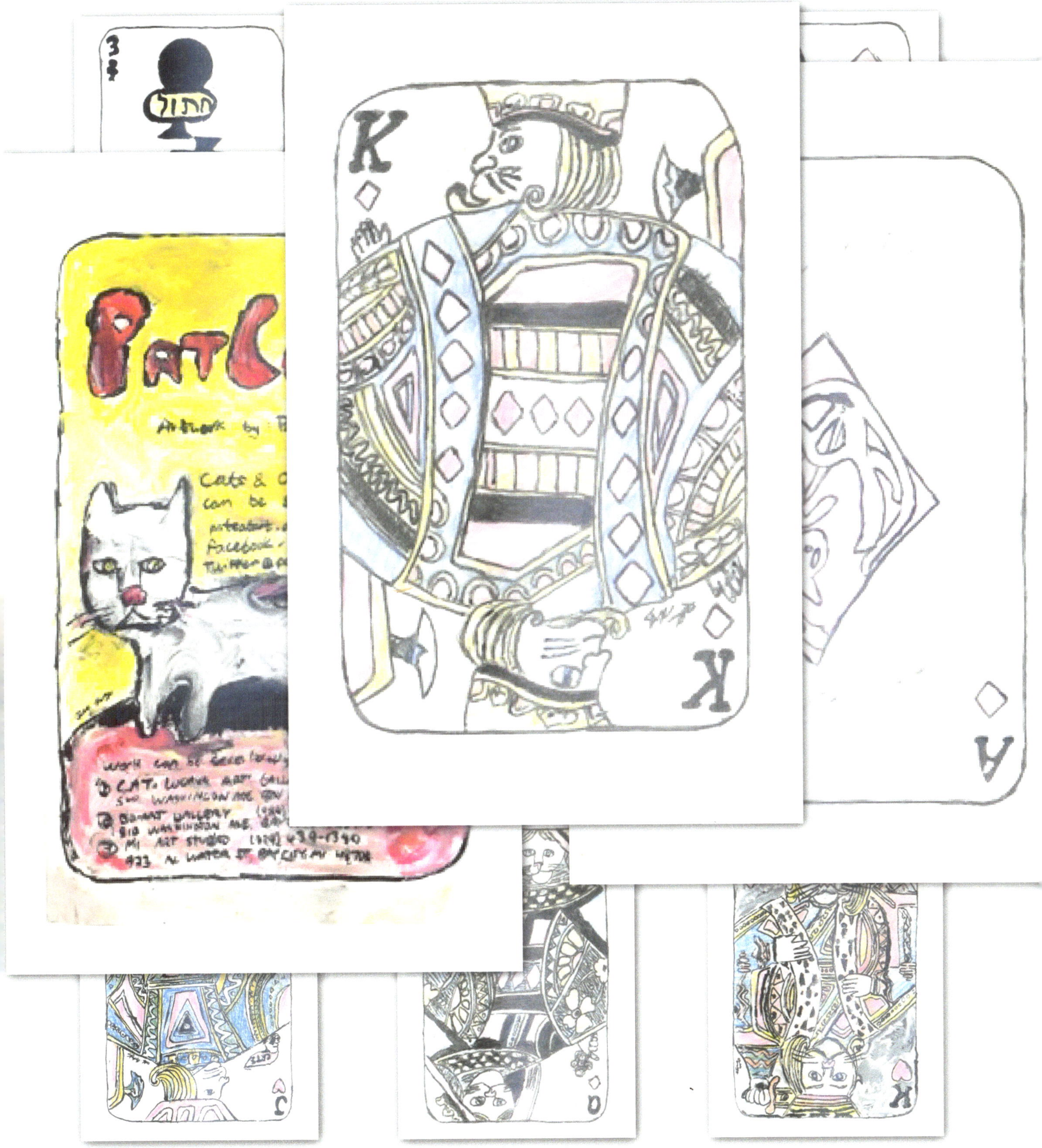

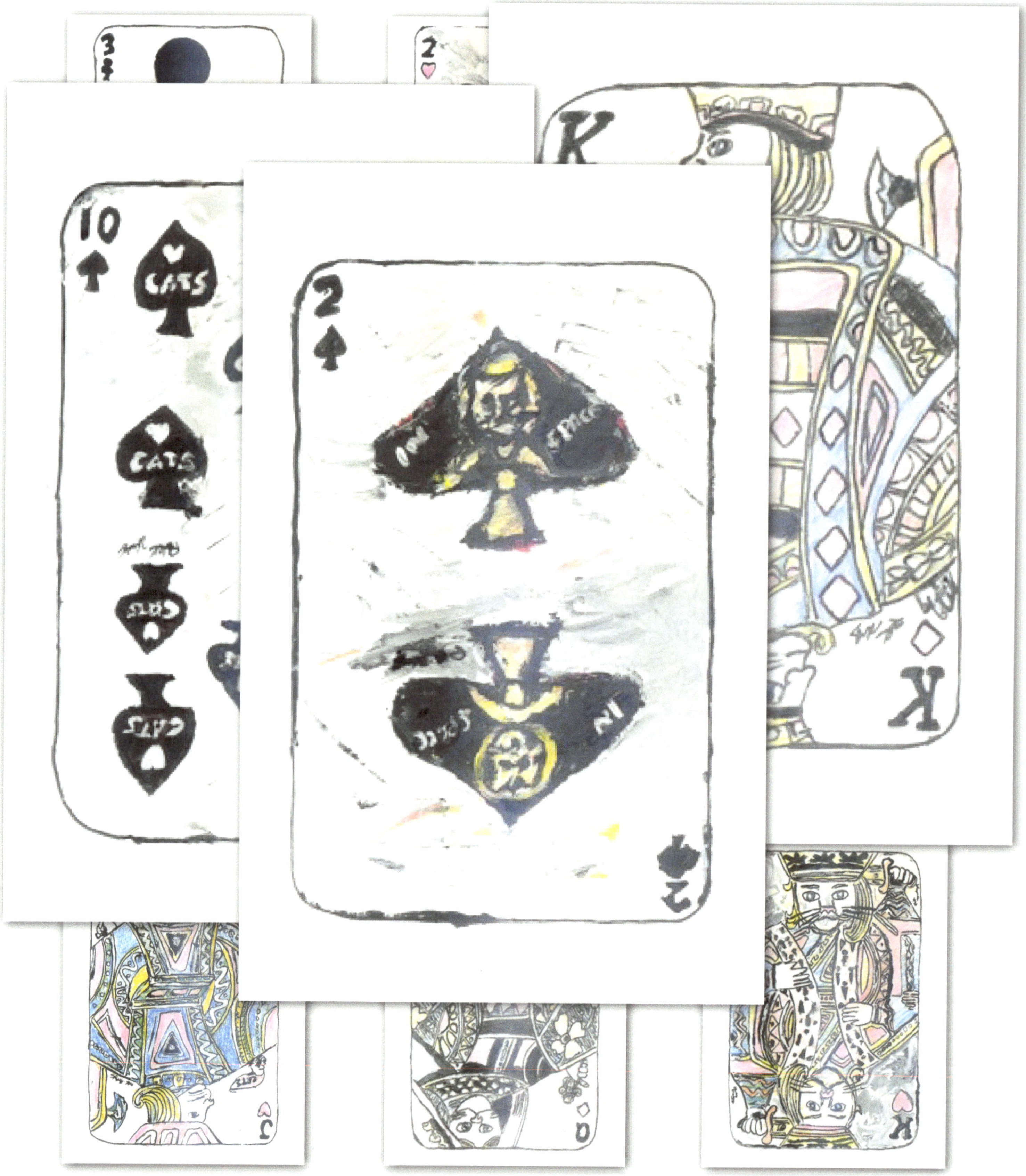

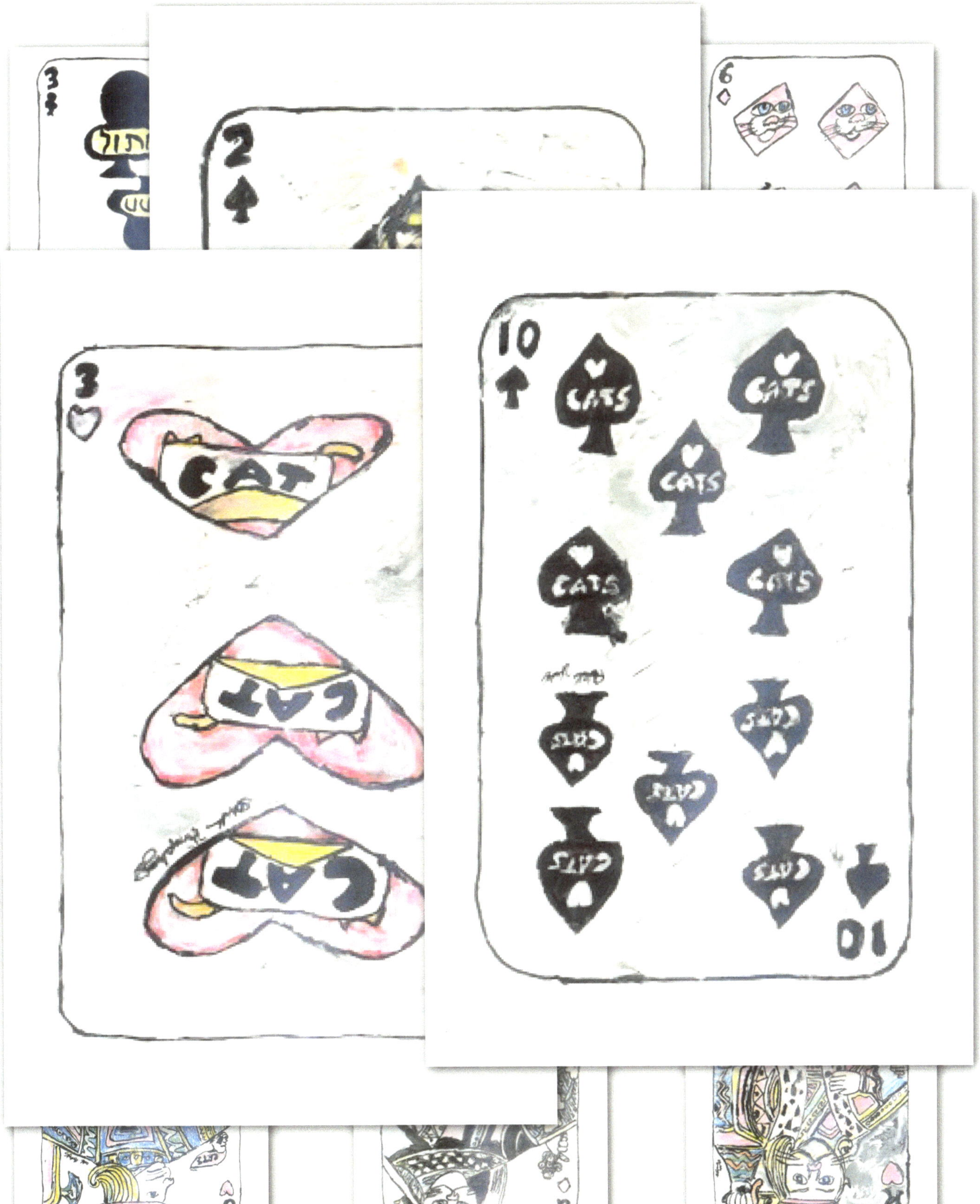
3
CAT
CAT
CAT
10
CATS
CATS
CATS
CATS
CATS
01

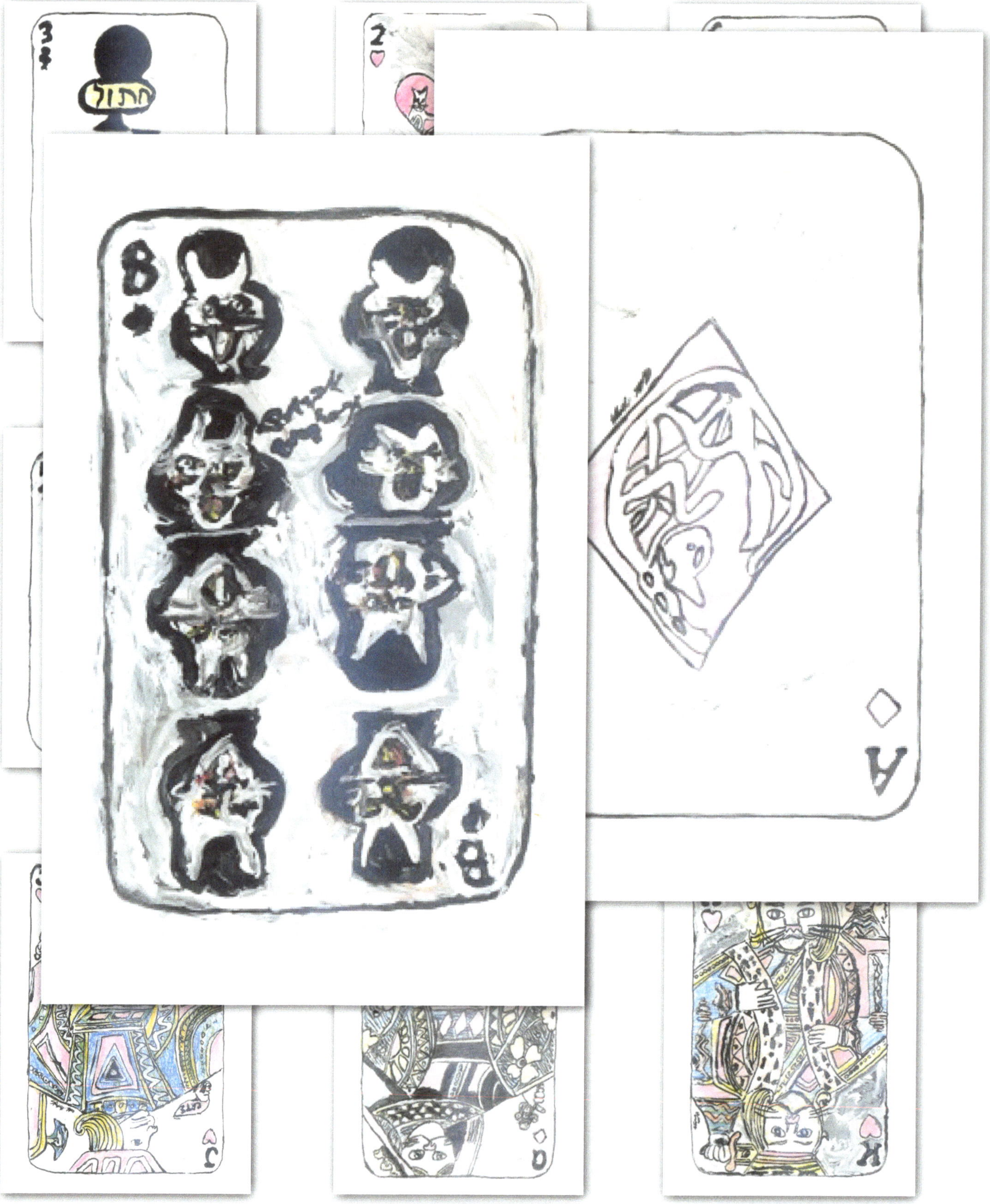

patcatart playing cards

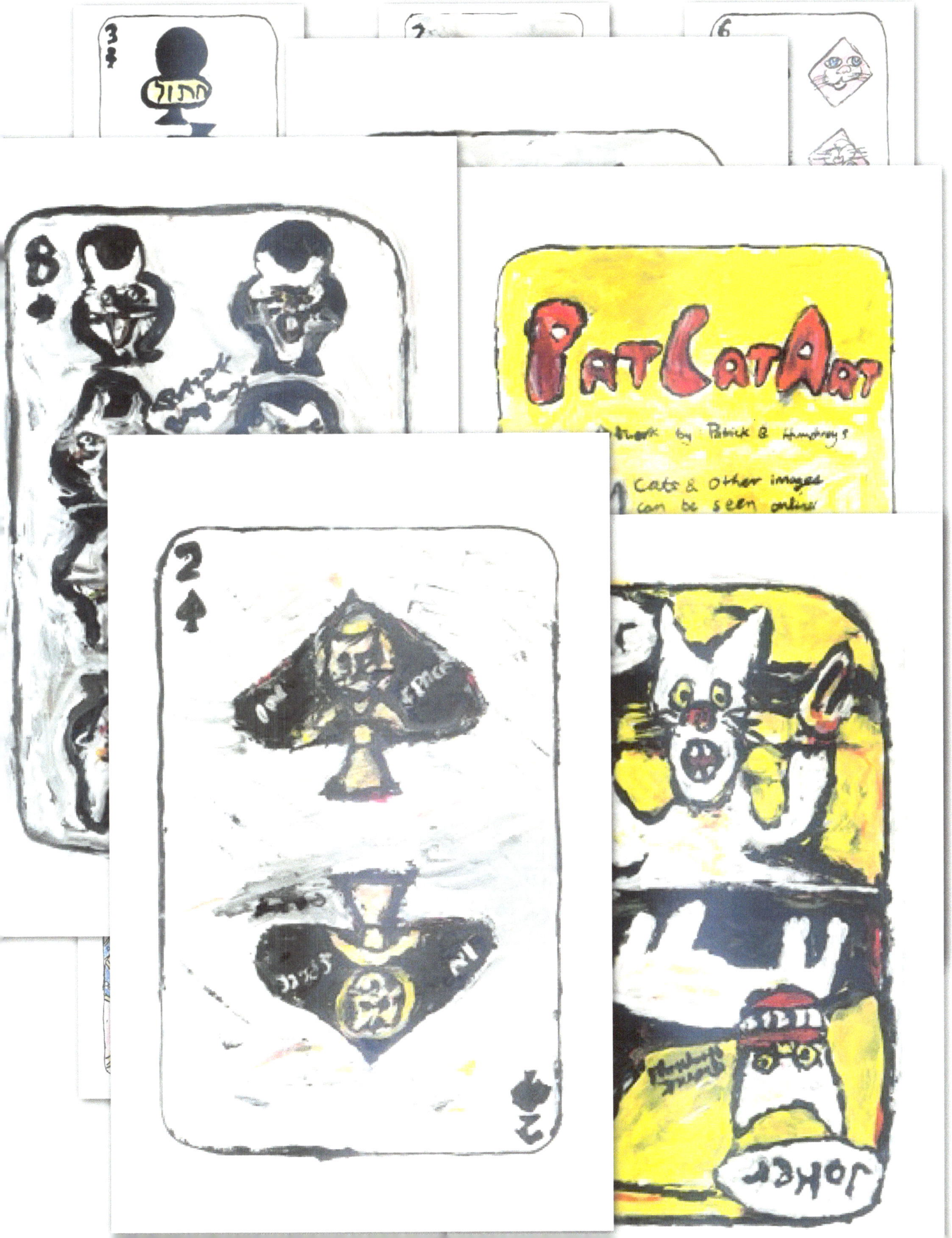

www.ingramcontent.com/pod-product-compliance
Lightning Source LLC
Chambersburg PA
CBHW050858180526
45159CB00007B/2715
* 9 7 8 1 5 0 3 0 7 7 8 8 1 *